About the Author

Ra el Bridge is the author of six bestselling books about
pe al development, smart thinking and entrepreneurship,
in ing *Ambition: Why It's Good To Want More and How To
Get   and How to Start a Business Without Any Money. Already
bri.. it* is her seventh book. She is the former Enterprise
. . of *The Sunday Times* and has taken two solo shows
 . Edinburgh Fringe Festival. She has an MA degree in
 . omics from Cambridge University.

ALREADY

Brilliant

Play to your strengths in work and life

RACHEL BRIDGE

piatkus

PIATKUS

First published in Great Britain in 2018 by Piatkus

1 3 5 7 9 10 8 6 4 2

A CIP catalogue record for this book
is available from the British Library.

ISBN 978-0-349-41734-9

Typeset in Stone Serif by M Rules
Printed and bound in Great Britain by
Clays Ltd, St Ives plc

Papers used by Piatkus are from well-managed forests
and other responsible sources.

MIX
Paper from
responsible sources
FSC® C104740
FSC
www.fsc.org

Piatkus
An imprint of
Little, Brown Book Group
Carmelite House
50 Victoria Embankment
London EC4Y 0DZ

An Hachette UK Company
www.hachette.co.uk

www.improvementzone.co.uk

For Jack and Harry

Contents

Introduction   1

1   Start facing in the right direction   7

2   Draw your own map   23

3   Identify your strengths   39

4   Decide how you work best   57

5   Don't let anything hold you back   67

6   Begin developing good habits   87

7   Start thinking in a different way   101

8   Start taking control   111

9   Now add the magic ingredients   123

10   Take the first step   135

11   Keep it real   147

12   Start getting excited   159

13   Ten powerful ideas to help you on your way   169

14   What now?   179

Acknowledgements   181

Index   183

Introduction

'What day is it?', asked Winnie the Pooh. 'It's today,'
squeaked Piglet. 'My favourite day,' said Pooh

Winnie the Pooh, **A.A. Milne**

What's the first thought that goes through your mind when you wake up in the morning? Do you jump out of bed in excitement looking forward to the day and all the interesting things you are going to be doing; or do you pull the duvet over your head in dread at the thought of the long, dull hours ahead of you?

If the second version is the one you recognise, you are not alone. The sad truth is that many people spend their days doing jobs they hate, pursuing careers they are not suited for, living lives that don't make them happy. A recent survey of workers by a recruitment firm found that a third of participants were bored in their jobs, while almost half confessed to leaving part of their true selves behind when they set off for work in the morning. Every day the same relentless routine of fighting for a seat on the train to get to and from work, or queuing for the bus in the rain, with only the brief respite of evenings, weekends and holidays to relieve the tedium.

The crazy thing is that you probably have no shortage of wonderful things you'd like to do. That glittering new career. That big promotion. That exciting new life in the sun. That book you want to write, that business you want to start, that amazing idea you long to put into action.

The problem is that achieving any of those goals feels just so impossible and out of reach. Maybe you feel you lack the skills to improve your situation. Or perhaps it feels as though there are too many obstacles standing in your way to achieve your goals. Maybe you are simply unhappy with what you are doing and are not really sure why. Perhaps you struggle to even find the time to understand what it is that you want to do.

Perhaps you just don't know where to start.

So instead you live your life through Google, clicking on houses you can't afford, holidays you will never go on, places you will never visit, adventures you will never have.

Somehow you have found yourself in a rut and you can't find the way out. Your life and career have ended up miles away from where you had envisaged and you have no idea how to fix them and get them back on track.

The good news is that this book can help. It will help you work out what you want to do, and show you how to get there. It will explain how to start facing in the right direction, how to plan your route, and how to take control of the decisions that really matter.

Packed with practical tips and ideas, and interviews with successful people in all walks of life, and supported by academic research, it will show you how to find a way of working that suits you best, how to begin developing good habits and how to overcome any obstacles standing in your way. And even better, it will show you how to turn those obstacles into advantages that will help rather than hinder you.

Most importantly, this book will show you how to play to your strengths. You may not realise it, but your personality, character, experiences, skills and even your personal circumstances are all fantastic tools and assets that you can use to create the life and career you've always wanted – no matter who you are, where you live or what you currently do for a living.

Now, playing to your strengths is not some kind of vague feel-good idea; it is a very practical and pragmatic approach to achieving more. It means deliberately focusing on the things that you can already do and then making those things as good as they can be, rather than wasting your energy worrying about the things you can't do. It's about identifying and using the resources you already have, rather than pointlessly trying to improve the bits that aren't that great, in the futile hope of being amazing at everything.

It is an approach that makes a lot of sense. You have limited time and energy in life, so it is far more effective to use those to build up your strengths, where you already have some ability, rather than trying to improve your weaknesses, where you don't.

That's because – and it is important to remember this – to get ahead in work and life you don't actually need to be good at everything; you just need to be good at some things, and then to use those skills in the most effective way.

What's more, using your strengths can not only help you get to where you want to be, it can also improve how you feel. A recent study by academic psychologists found that people who felt they were using their strengths regularly developed greater levels of well-being over time than those who did not, measured in terms of greater self-esteem and vitality, and lower stress levels.

But while focusing on improving your positive qualities might sound obvious, it's actually the complete opposite of how we usually operate in life. Assessments and reports at school and work typically focus on the things we need to improve, not the things we are already good at.

Remember all those 'could do better' and 'room for improvement' comments in your school reports? Of course you do. From a young age we are conditioned to pay as much attention to our weaknesses as our strengths, which means that inevitably those are the things we tend to dwell on. Studies show that if people are given a report that highlights four strengths and one weakness, it is the single weakness they remember most.

It's hardly surprising, then, that so many people doubt themselves and question their abilities. Well, not anymore. It's time to start thinking in a different way.

This book looks at how to play to your strengths in both work and life because the two have become increasingly entwined. Forget the traditional nine-to-five working day – for many people this has become the eight-to-six or even the seven-to-seven, and even this distinction has become increasingly blurred as smartphones, apps and emails mean that the demands of work creep into other parts of our day.

At the same time advances in technology have brought with them a new flexibility, which can allow us to work in new ways, perhaps working for ourselves, or working remotely or even starting a business in our spare time. This flexibility can also give you the freedom to take time away from work to travel or pursue other interests for a while, without fear that you have irredeemably cut off your route back into the workplace.

Either way, it has become increasingly hard to see where work ends and where the rest of your life begins. And this means that it makes sense to take a holistic approach to living a better life.

So, here's the good news. You don't have to stay stuck in your rut, watching your life go by as the days turn into weeks and then into years. You don't have to live with the choices you have made. You can start afresh and make the changes you need, to get to where you want to be.

That's because you are capable of much more than you think. You already have the seeds of your success inside you. It's all right there, just waiting for you to press the start button.

Let's get going.

Chapter 1

Start facing in the right direction

'Wherever you go, go with all your heart'
Confucius, philosopher

There is a place in London called Kidzania, which has been kitted out as an indoor child-sized city. Here, children aged four to 14 can try out their dream job for the day. They might decide to be a pilot or fire fighter, present a radio show or work in a bank. There is a child-sized bank, hospital, police station and fire station, as well as an advertising agency, a cleaning company, an estate agency, an animation studio, a hotel, a newspaper and a theatre. Children are paid for the activities they do with pretend money called KidZos, which they can take as cash or as a credit on pretend debit cards and use to buy toys and sweets.

How brilliant it would be if there were a place like this for adults, where you could try out lots of alternative lives to find out where your true strengths and interests lie, safe in the knowledge that if you didn't like one life you could immediately switch to another one with no cost or penalty. You could test out whether being a circus performer would suit you better than being a lawyer, perhaps; or find out whether being a helicopter pilot is as much fun as it seems.

The hardest part about feeling stuck in a rut and being frustrated with your current situation is that it can be daunting to know what to do instead. There are so many different jobs you could potentially be doing that it is not always immediately obvious what a better alternative might be. Having a ready-made place to try out alternatives would be a great solution.

Sadly such a place does not yet exist. Fortunately, however, there are a number of tools you can use to work out where you'd like to be heading – and what direction you should be facing in to get there. Let's take a look.

Go back to basics

Start by asking yourself some questions. What would your ideal life look like? What kind of place would you want to live in, what kind of job would you like to be doing? What sorts of activities would you like to do in your spare time? How important is it to you to be busy, or creative, or well paid, or famous, or well respected by your peers? What priority do you place on having a job that fits around your family? Would you prefer to work on your own or as part of a team?

Here are some of the types of goal you might choose to aim for:

Career goals Your aim might be to get a promotion at work giving you more responsibility, more leadership opportunities and greater freedom to make decisions. Or it might be pursuing an entirely different career to the one you currently have.

Work goals Your goal might be to start working for yourself, or to start your own business. Or it might be finding a way to be able to earn a living from doing something you love.

Personal goals You might have a particular personal project that you would like to achieve – learning how to make bread, raising pigs, trekking across the Andes, writing a book.

Lifestyle goals You might wish to live your day-to-day life in a certain way – moving to a different country, perhaps, or living in a more environmentally aware way, or adopting a simpler lifestyle. Or your aim might be to achieve a better work–life balance.

Creative goals You might have a yearning to start being more creative in some way – to build your own house, or learn how to paint, or create a vegetable garden, or start writing poetry.

Whatever you think your ideal life and career might look like, now is the time to start giving it some shape.

Question everything

In every area of your life, start asking: Why? Why not? What happens if? Why do you do the job you do, why do you live where you do, why do you wear the clothes you wear, why do you eat the food you do? What decisions did you take, and what assumptions did you make, that got you to where you are now?

It is so easy to just sleepwalk through life without ever really stopping to think what you are doing, and why. But if you really want to make the most of who you are and what strengths you have, it can really help to understand how you got to the place you are today. And in particular to examine whether it was because of conscious decisions you made, or because you let other people make decisions for you.

When I needed a new kitchen, the salesman in the showroom proudly showed me his firm's latest innovation – a secret cutlery drawer. It was hidden within one of the large pan drawers so that when the pan drawer was closed there was no way of knowing that the cutlery drawer was inside. I was impressed, I was persuaded, I bought one. A secret cutlery drawer, I thought, what a brilliant idea, how did I ever survive without one?

But, when my new kitchen was installed, I suddenly realised that having a secret cutlery drawer is the most ridiculous idea ever. Why would you want your cutlery drawer to be secret? It makes no sense for it to be hidden away out of sight. In fact quite the opposite. You want visitors, family and friends to be able to find your cutlery drawer, on their own, as quickly as possible, without you constantly having to show them where it is. You don't want to have to draw them a map.

So now I am stuck with my stupid secret cutlery drawer; the only upside being that every time I open it, it reminds me very forcefully to think for myself next time anyone tries to sell me anything else completely pointless.

Question the choices you make because this will help you set your direction and make it easier to understand what might be consciously holding you back.

Assess your reactions

A simple way to find out what you'd really like to do is to see how you react to other people's stories of their lives. There was a story in a newspaper not long ago about Geraldine Forster, a 72-year-old British woman who has decided to spend her retirement backpacking her way around the world. She has so far spent seven years away from home with nothing but a backpack, laptop and camera, travelling round Asia, Russia, Australia, Europe and the USA, and doing voluntary work in the Philippines, Cambodia and Thailand.

She lives very frugally, paying for her travels with the money she receives from her pension, and often spends only £5 a night for a shared dormitory room in a backpackers' hostel and 40 pence for a plate of food from a street market. So far she has been to more than 50 countries and comes back to the UK and Spain only once or twice a year to visit her children and grandchildren. As she travels she posts photos and stories on her website Backpacker Granny (www.backpackergranny.com) and hopes one day to start running Backpacker Granny tours.

The article quoted her saying, 'You may think I'm crazy, but I'm single, I have my pension and I believe we can do incredible things once we realise the only boundaries are those we set ourselves. Budget travel makes me feel truly alive. I don't hanker after air-conditioning, white fluffy towels or room service. That's just soulless. I have absolutely no plans to stop, or even soften up. I want this way of life to continue for ever.'

But just as interesting as the story itself were the readers' comments underneath the article, which were completely split. Half of them were from people saying how envious they were of her and how much they would love to live her way themselves. As one said, 'I hope I'm like her when I retire. Life is for living.'

However, the other comments were from people saying how they couldn't understand the appeal of it at all and would much rather stay at home. One said, 'No way. Each to their own.' Another said, 'I prefer the comforts of home and family.' Another said, 'It's OK when you're young but as I get older I appreciate the comfort of a good hotel, air-conditioning and a G&T.'

What would your comment have been? Would you choose to live that way? And, more broadly, what value do you place on experiences compared with material possessions and creature comforts? There are no right or wrong answers to those questions, but it can be useful to monitor your own reactions to stories like this one, because it gives you a better idea of what really matters to you and where your priorities lie. That can really help to determine the direction you need to be heading in.

Explore your interests

The simplest way to reset the direction you're going in is to find something you love doing – and then do everything you can to keep on doing it in some way. That might mean working in it, volunteering in it, or studying it.

Fuchsia Dunlop first became interested in China when she was working at the BBC Monitoring Unit, editing transcripts from foreign media broadcasts in the Asia Pacific region. As soon as she could take some time off, she went backpacking to China for a month on her own. She loved it and when she got back she began taking weekly evening classes to learn Mandarin. Then, encouraged by a colleague, she applied for and won a British Council scholarship to study history at Sichuan University in Chengdu for a year.

The experience changed her life. While Fuchsia was in China, she became interested in Chinese cooking and in particular in Sichuanese cuisine. She started taking lessons at a provincial cookery school in her spare time and when her British Council scholarship ended, she stayed on in China to study full time at the cookery school when they invited her to join their three-month chef's training course. It was a big privilege as no foreigner had ever been invited to do this before, making her the first Western woman to be taught Sichuanese cooking. The school even let her pay the local student rate of about £100.

When Fuchsia returned to London, her friends suggested that she go back to the BBC and embark on a proper career there, but she had other ideas. She began reviewing Chinese restaurants for *Time Out* magazine and wrote a cookbook about Sichuanese food. When her book, *Sichuan Cookery*, was published in 2001 it attracted a huge amount of attention, because it was probably the first regional Chinese cookbook written in English that had been researched on the ground in China. It was hailed as an instant classic and is often included in lists of the best cookbooks of all time.

Fuchsia has now written five books about Chinese food and culinary culture, including her memoir *Shark's Fin and Sichuan Pepper*, and spends up to three months in China each year. She appears on radio and television, is a consultant to Sichuan restaurants in London, teaches Chinese cookery to companies such as Marks and Spencer, and leads food tours to China. Her love of China, and Chinese food, has become a fully fledged career.

She says, 'I have never had a career plan. My objective in life wasn't to make loads of money, it was to do interesting things. I have been lucky to find something that other people are interested in too. I find it an amazing thought that there are all these people cooking my recipes from my books. There are a lot of people who don't do what they want to do and who feel miserable and regretful, so if you can do what you want to do and make it work, it is very satisfying.'

KNOWHOW

If you are interested in studying in a university abroad, the British Council (www.britishcouncil.org) runs programmes to several countries, including Japan, Azerbaijan, Brazil and India, as well as China. Some of these programmes come with scholarships to cover tuition and living expenses. Their Generation UK-China scholarship programme, for example, offers 100 current or recent graduates the opportunity to study in one of ten Chinese universities for up to 11 months and covers all basic living needs, including tuition fees, accommodation and a monthly living allowance.

Do some job shadowing

If you have a friend or even a friend-of-a-friend who is doing a job you think you might be interested in, ask them if you can shadow them at work for a few hours, or even a day.

When I was in my early twenties and wondering what kind of career to pursue, I decided fairly randomly that I might like to be a producer for the BBC. I didn't really have any idea what the job actually entailed, I just rather liked the idea of sitting in a van somewhere doing outside broadcasts while drinking lots of tea. Fortunately, I had a friend who was already on the BBC's technical training course learning how to be a producer so he let me follow him round for a morning, showing me the kinds of thing that a producer would spend their days doing. It all looked very technical and fiddly, with most of the time spent in small rooms the size of cupboards with no windows and working with complicated machines that looked as though they could bite your fingers off. It didn't appeal to me at all. I thanked him for his time and immediately crossed being a BBC producer off my list.

If none of your friends does the sort of job you want to know about, start quizzing them about what their friends do, or what their parents do, and see if they will let you visit where they work. Even a half-hour visit to someone's office or workspace can be illuminating.

There's also a new service that will let you pay to job shadow someone for a few hours or more. For £60 and upwards Viewvo (www.viewvo.com) offers the opportunity to spend quality time with someone who is already doing a job that interests you. Options range from becoming a dog trainer to working in a theatre to setting up a vineyard. During your time with the person you are shadowing, you get to find out exactly what the work entails, and what the good and bad bits are. You also get a real insight into the important financial considerations, such as how much it would cost you to start up a business doing what they are doing and how much money can you realistically expect to make.

Look beyond your current surroundings

David Meakin was a grain trader for a large company in Wiltshire. He had always dreamed of becoming a farmer, but knew it would be almost impossible to buy his own farm in England because of the expense. However, after doing some research he realised that he could buy a 50-hectare farm in France for the same price as his semi-detached, three-bedroom house in Wiltshire.

So when he asked his girlfriend Sarah to marry him, the proposal came with a condition attached – she had to give up her job working for a credit card company and move to France with him. Fortunately, she said yes and after several trips to France, they found exactly what they were looking for in the Lot valley, near Cahors.

At first it was tough. They spent their first five weeks in France living in a tent while the paperwork to buy the farm was completed, and when they actually moved in, none of their furniture had arrived and there was no hot water. They also found it hard to communicate with the locals because neither of them could speak the language.

Sarah says, 'David was under a lot of pressure trying to make the farm work and he would yell at me because I couldn't drive the tractor in a straight line. We used to have these stand-up shouting matches. And when the phone rang, we would argue over who was going to answer it because we couldn't speak French.'

But they persevered and then came a turning point. As well as having extensive fields for wheat and barley, the farm came with five hectares of vines. Although the couple had no experience of making wine, they suddenly realised it was an opportunity to see what they could do.

Sarah says, 'The only thing we knew about wine was how to buy it in Sainsbury's, but we couldn't just ignore the vines and hope they would go away, so we decided we had to do something with them. People thought we were mad. Even we thought we were mad.'

Indeed they knew so little about making wine that a friendly English winemaker had to fax them daily instructions on what to do. The first time Sarah and David tried to sell their wine at the village festival, they sold just nine bottles.

But they realised that their wine was good, so instead of quitting, they entered their first vintage, a 1994 Cabernet Franc, in the renowned Guide Hachette wine competition. It won two stars. Encouraged by their early success, they decided to focus their time and energy on winemaking, deliberately using as few chemicals as possible.

The effort has paid off. More than 23 years after they first arrived in France, they are still there and their Domaine du Merchien vineyard, which is now certified organic, sells up to 25,000 bottles of red and rosé wine a year. They sell their wine partly from a stall in the market and partly through a membership scheme they set up, called Partners in Wine, in which customers lease a row of vines in return for a guaranteed number of bottles.

They have also expanded into making beer, having built a brewery on site, and sell 20,000 bottles a year. Their two children went to the local French school and are now both bilingual, with one studying law at university in France.

David, now 55, says, 'Who could want for better than this? I was always envious of people who were content in their jobs and now I am like that myself.' Sarah adds, 'I feel so pleased with what we have managed to do. No one can ever take that away from us.'

Underpin it

Whatever your goal is, make sure that something solid underpins it. In particular beware of 'achieving wealth and fame' becoming your sole aim. Your chances of being happy as well as successful will be considerably improved if you can pick goals that have a more substantial purpose as their foundation.

In 2009 a group of researchers at the University of Rochester in the USA conducted a study to discover what types of goal led to a happier life. They interviewed 147 college graduates and asked them to rate certain goals in order of importance. The goals were divided into two groups: intrinsic purpose-driven goals, such as having deep, enduring relationships, helping others improve their lives, growing and learning new things and being physically healthy; and extrinsic, profit-led goals, such as being a wealthy person, being admired by many people and achieving a desired look.

The researchers then interviewed the graduates again a year later and compared the level of importance the students had placed on achieving these different types of goal with their level of well-being, as measured by their satisfaction in life, self-esteem, anxiety, physical signs of stress, and level of positive and negative emotions.

The study found that those graduates who had placed greater importance on achieving intrinsic, purpose-driven goals reported much higher levels of satisfaction and self-esteem and lower levels of anxiety and depression than those who had placed the most importance on extrinsic, profit-led goals.

Edward Deci, one of the researchers, said, 'Even though our culture puts a strong emphasis on attaining wealth and fame, pursuing these goals does not contribute to having a satisfying life. The things that make your life happy are growing as an individual, having loving relationships and contributing to your community.'

Own it

Sometimes it can feel as though everything interesting and exciting in the world has already been done by someone else before you. It's not for nothing that the phrase 'Been there, done that, got the T-shirt' is so popular. When I told a friend I would love to go and visit Bali one day, she just rolled her eyes and said, 'But Bali is so OVER.'

But you are the only one living your life and you should never forget that. Your experiences matter to you precisely because they are yours, and living your life through other people's experiences makes no sense at all.

When YouTube stars Joe Suggs and Caspar Lee decided to go on a road trip across the USA and make a film about it, they had one problem – they felt as though the idea has been done many times before. In the beginning scenes of their film *Joe and Caspar's Road Trip USA*, they are filmed having a meeting with a producer who excitedly tells them about the trip he has planned for them.

Joe says dismissively, 'It's been done so many times.' However, the producer merely responds, 'But not with you two in it.'

He's right. Never forget that you are on your own personal road trip through life. It's yours. Own it.

Don't be afraid to change direction

It can be hard to switch to another path in life if you are already doing well on the path you are on. Not only do you have to deal with your own fears that your new direction may not work out, you also have to deal with everyone else's incomprehension, disappointment or even resentment about what you are trying to do. But it will be worth it.

For many years Henry Naylor was a highly successful comedy writer. Having met his comedy writing partner Andy Parsons at university, the two of them started out writing sketches for Mel Smith and Griff Rhys Jones before getting a show of their own, *Parsons and Naylor's Pull-Out Sections*, on Radio 2. Henry also wrote for the satirical puppet show *Spitting Image* and for several years played Rowan Atkinson's sidekick Bough in television commercials for Barclaycard.

But despite his success, Henry began to realise that he wanted to tackle more serious subjects, in particular the impact that war had on ordinary people. He says, 'I wanted to write something about the disparity between what journalists see and what they actually put out on air.'

He was at home watching the news one day when he saw a BBC newsman being blown off his chair by a bomb in a makeshift studio in Afghanistan. Seconds later he saw the cameraman running in front of the camera and realised that it was an old friend.

When the war was over, Henry got in touch with his friend and asked him if he could explain what it was like to be a war correspondent. Rather than talking, though, the friend invited Henry to come out to Kabul to see for himself. So Henry flew out there with a photographer and spent ten days being shown around. He says, 'It completely changed my life. Suddenly I was going round refugee camps, I was going round landmine victims' camps, I was meeting women who had been tortured by the Taliban. It made me realise that there were human stories in the news that couldn't be conveyed by journalists because they only tend to deal with the big events.'

Henry came home knowing that instead of writing jokes,

he wanted to write serious hard-hitting plays that told the human stories that go unreported in the news. Having established such a strong career in comedy, however, it was a bold move. He says, 'It was liberating to be able to write in my own voice and find my own form of self-expression. But it was also extremely frightening because you have nowhere to hide if it's rubbish.'

He finished writing his first play, *The Collector*, about the occupying forces in Iraq, and put it on at the Edinburgh Fringe Festival in 2014. But the first night did not go well and a reviewer was horrible about it, suggesting that Henry had overstepped the mark by thinking he could write a serious play. The play also initially got a confused reaction from audiences that had come along expecting to see a comedy. But after two days the play came together and a reviewer from the *Scotsman* newspaper loved it. By the end of the festival *The Collector* had won a Fringe First for new writing, one of the most coveted awards at the festival.

Henry has since written a new play every year for the Edinburgh Fringe, all covering different aspects of war in the Middle East. All of them have won awards and much critical acclaim, including from *The Times* theatre critic, who wrote, 'Naylor is emerging as one of our best new playwrights.' Henry's plays are now performed in theatres around the world and he plans to turn his play *Angel* into a film.

He says, 'Changing my direction is the best thing I have ever done. It feels fantastic. I have got a bit of fire in my belly. With my plays I am genuinely trying to express something, and that is better and more rewarding than anything I have ever done.'

It can be easy to feel that you have to stick with the job you are doing, even if you don't like it that much, because it feels a lot safer than venturing into the unknown and trying something new or different. And if you are extremely good at doing your job, it can be a hundred times harder because it feels as though you have so much more to lose.

But just because you are really good at something doesn't mean you have to keep on doing it. There's no limit to what you can be good at. In fact once you give yourself permission to try, you could find that you are really good at lots of different jobs, and one of them might make you a lot more happy and fulfilled than you are at the moment.

NOW TAKE ACTION

1. Write down the three things that interest you most in life. They might be activities, pursuits, places, people, subjects, countries, anything. If it's something you'd like to be occupying a bigger part of your life, write it down.

2. Look at your list. Is there any way of making a living from any of these three interests? Or of spending more time doing them? Or of combining them in an interesting way?

3. Identify any friends, family members or work colleagues who might support you in your mission to make changes in your life. It can be really nice to have someone to chat through your ideas with, but make sure they are someone you trust.

———————

Chapter 2

Draw your own map

'The people who get on in this world are the people who get up and look for the circumstances they want, and, if they can't find them, make them'

George Bernard Shaw, playwright

Sometimes it can feel as though life is a series of escalators, and that if you don't get on the right one at the right time, you will get left behind and permanently miss out. That if you don't study this subject at this time and live here and do this job and then that job, then you will never get to where you want to be. But in reality life is much more fluid, and happily it's becoming increasingly so. You don't have to take the escalator, you can take the stairs instead. Or the lift. Or do a combination of all three. There are all kinds of ways of getting to where you want to be – and the route you take is very much in your control.

Steve Jobs, the founder of technology firm Apple, understood this. He said, 'Life can be much broader once you discover one simple fact, and that is: everything around you that you call life was made up by people that were no smarter than you. And you can change it, you can influence it, you can build your own things that other people can use . . . Once you learn that, you'll never be the same again.'

So now that you've discovered the new direction you want to go in, the next step is to choose how you want to move towards it. Take a deep breath and breathe out slowly, because this is where you get to taste the freedom you've longed for. You don't have to follow a set route to get to your goal, and you don't have to do things in any particular order.

Sometimes the route you choose to take might not be the most direct path. For example, you may prefer to take the scenic route that takes in the view and winds through lots of interesting places along the way. Or you might decide to take the direct route that is really hard-going and challenging in places, but gets you there quicker. Either way is completely fine. It's your life, and it's your route.

The people who get the most out of life are not the ones who unthinkingly plod along a well-trodden path that so many people have taken before them. Rather, they are the ones who decide to do things a bit differently. They are the ones who say, 'But what happens if I try it this way, or that way?'

Let's take a look at how to do this.

Start with a blank sheet of paper

There are a couple of really dangerous words in the English language that can do an enormous amount of damage if they end up in the wrong hands. One of those words is 'ought' and the other one is 'should'. As in, you ought to be doing it this way and you really should be doing it that way.

But you don't have to follow the rules, and you don't have

to carry all the old bits of your life with you and try to make them fit. You can pick and choose the things you still want, and leave the rest behind. If living in London or working in accountancy, for example, are no longer right for you, then now is the moment to ditch them and start afresh.

Think about what you would do if you could start from scratch without anything already in place. How would you spend your time? Where would you live? What kind of day-to-day life would you lead? What kind of balance would you choose between work and free time? Once you begin to let your imagination run free without restraint, that's when your true path will start to emerge. And that's when it gets really exciting.

This is exactly what Mario Salcedo did. In 1996 at the age of 48 he left his job as director of international finance for a multinational corporation with the aim of embarking on a completely new way of living. He had two goals – he wanted to work for himself and he wanted to travel the world. He decided the best way to achieve both would be to live on a cruise ship. So after taking more than a hundred cruises with different lines, he opted to base his new life on Royal Caribbean's ships.

Mario has now lived on their cruise ships virtually full time for more than 20 years, equivalent to more than 900 cruises. He always chooses the cheapest cabin to save on costs and runs his business managing investment portfolios for high-net-worth individuals from a laptop, working at a table by the pool from 7am until 2pm each day.

Indeed he has become such a familiar presence that the crew erected a sign above his table that reads, 'Super Mario's Office'.

He spends the rest of his time scuba diving and chatting to other passengers. He spends six months a year on one ship, six months on another, and only two weeks on land between voyages, when he visits a doctor and dentist for a check-up.

It's obviously not a lifestyle that many people could afford to emulate, but at a total cost of about £4,800 a month, it costs him only as much as it would to rent a two-bedroom flat in the London Borough of Kensington and Chelsea, and he has no food or household bills, or entertainment, transport, holiday or travel costs to pay on top.

He told one magazine, 'I feel better at 66 than I did in the corporate rat race in my thirties. I'll keep cruising as long as I'm healthy and as long as I'm having fun. I'm probably the happiest person in the world.'

Give yourself the freedom to create your own route to your ideal life. You may have to modify bits of it as you go along to fit your budget or circumstances, but if you can at least set out knowing you have the freedom to shape the journey, that's a very good start.

Notice what your actions are telling you

Actions often speak louder than words, so take a look at what yours are trying to tell you. They may have a far clearer message to give you than your reason or logic can, about what you really want to be doing with your life.

My friend Jane is forever claiming that she wants to write a screenplay, but whenever she gets any spare time to write, she doesn't use to it write her screenplay, but spends it writing a brilliantly funny blog about how she never has the time or motivation to write her screenplay. She's now written many blogs and has attracted lots of followers, but her screenplay remains just an idea.

It does not take a rocket scientist to work out that Jane would perhaps be better off devoting her energies to writing her blog, possibly even ultimately turning it into a screenplay itself, rather than forcing herself to try to write her elusive screenplay, because the blog is so clearly what she enjoys doing most. Infuriatingly, though, she can't see it.

If you are forever saying that you want to do one thing but consistently do another thing that takes up the same amount of time and energy, perhaps it is time for a rethink. Stop standing in your own way. Look at what your actions are trying to tell you and take your lead from there.

Do something you enjoy

One of the secrets to achieving a fulfilling life is really simple: make sure you are engaged in activities that you enjoy. There's no point becoming a world-class trumpeter if you don't actually like playing the trumpet. The whole point of drawing your own map is that you can redesign your life around doing something you love. And because you like doing it, the chances are that you may get pretty good at it.

One day in 2008 five college friends from Texas A&M University in the USA started throwing balls into a basketball hoop in the backyard of the house they shared. Then one of them bet another one a sandwich that they couldn't nail a difficult shot. He managed it, and they all began to try to outdo each other with trick shots. As they became increasingly ambitious with their shots they began filming them on a video camera. When they watched it back later they thought it looked so funny they created a three-minute video and uploaded it onto YouTube, calling themselves Dude Perfect.

News of their trick shots spread and within a week their

YouTube video had got 100,000 views. As the number of views continued to rise, television and radio stations began to get in touch to see if they could interview the Dude Perfect team. Buoyed by the enthusiastic response to what they had done, the five of them began to make more videos of tricky basketball shots, including a 70-yard shot from the top of the stands at their university football stadium, which they called 'The World's Longest Basketball Shot'.

That shot led to more television appearances, sponsors and a huge number of followers on social media – and suddenly Dude Perfect had become a brand and a full-time job for the five of them. Dude Perfect (www.dudeperfect.com) now has more than 15.9 million subscribers, making it one of the most successful brands to have started on YouTube, and is estimated to be worth US $5 million. It has its own TV show and is sponsored by brands such as Nerf and Pringles. The team even has its own huge indoor arena to try out the shots. Their original video has been seen more than 17.8 million times.

It has been an incredible success story, particularly because that success has happened in such a short amount of time. As Tyler Toney, the one who took that first shot in the backyard, told an interviewer: 'It's been a really, really fun ride so far . . . I hope there's not an end date anytime soon.'

Of course, Dude Perfect makes it look easy and for most people simply doing what they enjoy is not automatically going to turn them into highly paid YouTube stars. While it would be nice to believe that tantalising phrase 'Do what you love and the money will follow', in reality it probably won't work out like that.

But thinking about how you might create a career around doing something you enjoy is a really good place to start, even if you need to tweak it a bit as you go along. The secret is to keep an open mind and be prepared to be a bit flexible. If you really love sport, for example, then make the decision to work within the sports industry – but stay open-minded about the kind of job and career you might have within it. You may not have the necessary talent to be a professional sportsperson, but you could still be the manager of a sports centre, or a sports journalist, or have a great career in sports marketing, or take up any one of a hundred roles involved in putting on a big sporting event.

KNOWHOW

If you would like to create a YouTube channel of your own, YouTube has set up a Creator Academy with tutorials on how to shoot and edit amazing videos, and how to build a business on YouTube and make money from your videos. Go to the YouTube website (www.youtube.com) and scroll down to the bottom to find the Creators hub.

Choose your own timing

Taking a gap year between school and starting work or university has becoming increasingly popular, to the extent that several companies have been set up solely to organise travel, temporary work and volunteering placements for young people setting off around the world.

But gap years don't have to be just for school leavers. There is no reason why you can't go on an adult gap year at a later stage of life – while changing jobs, perhaps, or after finishing some form of study, or when your children have left home. Jo Gardetta set off on an adult gap year at the age of 55 and at the time of writing has been travelling in Asia for more than a year with no plans to come home yet. She has travelled mostly on her own, making friends along the way, and in that time she has visited India, Thailand, Myanmar, Laos, Cambodia and Indonesia. She has also learnt to ride a scooter, been on a yoga retreat and swum in the Ganges. She has financed her trip by renting out her flat in London, by doing some freelance work editing scripts, which she used to do back home, and by living very frugally on a small budget.

She says, 'Nothing much was happening in my life. It wasn't a bad life – I had plenty of friends and lots to do, but it was the same stuff I'd been doing for the last few years and it dawned on me that I didn't actually need to be where I was. I was working as a freelance script editor and I realised that I could do this on my laptop in an Internet cafe in Goa just as easily as I could do it in an Internet cafe in Islington.'

The travelling has not just been fun; it has also opened up a whole raft of possibilities and opportunities. Jo is now planning to run art tours to India with an artist she met from New York, and has been offered a job running a guesthouse in Rajasthan. She says, 'I have learnt loads and loads of things. But mainly I've learnt that happiness doesn't come from outside things, places and people, it comes only from within.'

Taking time out can be a great way to recharge your batteries and give you a bit of breathing space to really think about what you want to achieve in your life, without distractions. You don't have to go abroad, or even travel – you might prefer to spend some focused time with your family or friends without the pressure of work. Whatever way you choose to spend it, time away from the workplace can really help you get a better perspective on what you'd like your life to look like.

To make the break effective, though, work out in advance how long you plan to take, what you plan to do with your time, and most importantly, how you plan to finance it. If you are currently in a job, for example, find out whether you could take some unpaid leave or a sabbatical for a few weeks or months, or even whether you could take all your annual holiday entitlement in one go. Or see if there is any way, like Jo did, of being able to take some work with you so you can finance your adventure as you go.

KNOWHOW

For ideas and guidance about how to take an adult gap year check out the following websites:
Gap360 (www.gap360.com) and
Travellers Worldwide (www.travellersworldwide.com).

Stop worrying about what other people think

You can't stop people talking about you. But you can stop caring so much. Don't waste time worrying about what other people think of the choices you make in life. One of the most liberating discoveries you can ever make is the realisation that deep down other people don't really care that much about what you do. They just like having something new to talk about for a while.

When Tony Gallagher announced he was going to work

in the kitchens of Moro, a highly regarded Spanish restaurant in London, after being sacked from his job as editor of the *Daily Telegraph*, the media couldn't get enough of the story, devoting many column inches to speculating about why he had made such a dramatic move. One Sunday newspaper devoted an entire page to the story. Most of the articles were condescending about his move, suggesting that Tony must have fallen very low to be doing such a menial job.

But Tony was the one who ended up having the last laugh. He had never intended to work at Moro for ever, but had simply realised he had an amazing opportunity to do something completely different before returning to journalism. He had a great time learning how to cook at his favourite restaurant and when he finished his stint there, he started a new job as the deputy editor of the *Daily Mail*.

In a piece he wrote afterwards, Tony said, 'This brief and tiny role attracted an inordinate amount of publicity – diarists, reviewers, an entire page in a Sunday broadsheet – because it was assumed this was my new career. There was an upsurge in visits by front-bench politicians, unable to disguise their schadenfreude at the sight of a newspaper editor brought low.' Instead, he said, he had been given 'the chance to enter a fantasy world, a sort of truncated gap year'. He added, 'It turned out to be the kind of experience that would have been impossible at cookery school.'

You too need to make sure you are not being held back by what other people might think. Ask the advice of friends, family and colleagues if you want, but then make up your own mind.

Adopt – and adapt – other people's good ideas

Good ideas can come from anywhere, so if you stumble across something that you like the sound of, think about how you might incorporate it into the path you want to take through life.

Findern Primary school, a rural school in Derbyshire, now allows its students to wear slippers in class after one of its teachers read about a study into the benefits of children taking their shoes off for lessons.

The ten-year study of 25 schools around the world, which was conducted by researchers at Bournemouth University, found that allowing pupils to remove their shoes improved their learning and helped them to do better in class. The study also looked at the impact on the academic results of the children up to university, and found there was a marked improvement compared with children who had been wearing shoes.

Since introducing the policy, the teachers at Findern Primary, which has 150 pupils aged from four to 11, have noticed an improvement in the children's behaviour, and now some of the teachers have even brought in their own slippers to wear.

Michelle Hall, the school's deputy head, told the local paper, 'It's been a huge success so far and even staff are wearing slippers in the classroom. Our pupils have always been well behaved, but we've noticed some changes. There is less stomping around and children are calmer and more relaxed. They love it.'

Thanks to traditional and social media, you have endless opportunities to hear about new ideas and different ways of doing things. Keep your ears tuned for stories that might be relevant to you. You could even consider cutting out useful articles and keeping a scrapbook of them to refer back to later.

KNOWHOW

Good ideas can come from anywhere. Consider buying a different magazine each month to one you might normally buy and see what ideas it sparks off when you read it. The retailer WHSmith (www. whsmith.co.uk) lists 1,158 magazines available to buy in the UK, from *The Artist* to *How it Works* magazine.

Write your own mission statement

A great way to describe the path you want to take in life is to write yourself a simple mission statement. A mission statement is a sentence that sums up your values and purpose and explains what you're about. Companies and brands often use mission statements as a way to explain the values that guide what they are trying to do – Starbucks' mission statement, for example, is 'to inspire and nurture the human spirit one person, one cup and one neighbourhood at a time'. Sony's is: 'To be a company that inspires and fulfils your curiosity.'

However, mission statements can also be a good way to think about what you stand for personally. Writing one for yourself will not only explain and describe where you are heading, it will also be an easy way to stay focused.

The most powerful way for you to benefit from a mission statement is to write one for a specific goal. If you are trying to get promoted at work, for example, your statement might be: 'Make sure my enthusiasm and expertise shine through every piece of work I do.'

If you are aiming to adopt a healthier way of life, your mission statement might be: 'Treat my body with care and respect in everything I do.'

Keep your statement as short as you can for maximum impact, and to make it easy to remember – the non-profit organisation TED's mission statement contains just three words: 'Ideas worth spreading.'

Keep your eye on the prize

Did you ever play that game when you were a child of walking blindfolded towards a tree? You look straight at the tree before you put the blindfold on, then once you have put the blindfold on you try to walk straight to it. It feels as though it should be easy, but when you rip off the blindfold after you have been walking for a while, you usually discover you are heading in a completely different direction.

It is scarily easy to get distracted from your goal, so you do need to make sure that you keep your eyes firmly fixed on it. Meandering your way towards it taking random paths and side roads is fine, but you must always stay focused on where you want to end up. Otherwise, you will probably go off track and end up somewhere else.

When she was growing up, my sister always wanted to be a journalist. At school and university, she wrote constantly for the school magazine and the university newspaper. Journalism was all she ever wanted to do. But when she graduated from university she needed to get a job to pay her debts and give her some money to live on, so she got the first job she could find, working as a waitress in a pizza restaurant. It was fine for a few weeks, but the weeks turned into months and she was still there. When my sister's friend Chris went to see her one day and asked how everything was going, she excitedly told him that the manager had offered her the opportunity to train as a pizza chef. Instead of sharing her excitement, however, Chris just looked at her in bemusement, and said, 'But I thought you wanted to be a journalist?'

In that moment my sister suddenly realised in horror that somehow, without meaning for it to happen, she had accidentally misplaced her dream. She quit her job in the pizza restaurant the following day and started applying for journalist positions. She soon landed a job as a reporter on a trade paper, which took her travelling around the world and led to her current job, as a correspondent on a national newspaper.

What dreams have you allowed to slip away? And, more importantly, can you find your way back to them?

NOW TAKE ACTION

1. Stop announcing your decisions or actions on Facebook or other social media, or even when you're talking to friends, and then waiting for people to comment on them. Unless you are genuinely seeking people's opinions, substantially limit the ways in which you allow people to comment on your life. Take ownership of your own direction.

2. Have a go at writing your own personal mission statement. What's the most important thing you need to remember about what you are trying to do?

3. If you are trying to make an important decision about what route to pursue, imagine having already chosen one option and then let it whirr away in the back of your mind for a few days. Now switch to another option and do the same. Keep going until you've thought about all the possible options you would be prepared to pursue. You will soon know which path feels like the right one for you.

————————

Chapter 3

Identify your strengths

'Knowing yourself is the beginning of all wisdom'
Aristotle, philosopher

B y now you should have a good idea of the goal you want to reach and the direction you want to go in. And you will have gained some understanding of how you might rearrange your life in order to achieve what you want. You may have decided that you want to retrain to enter a different profession, for example, in which case you need to start thinking about what qualifications you will need and where you will study for them.

Now it's time to identify the strengths you have that will help you get to where you want to be. Don't worry if you're not really sure what your strengths are right now; you're not the only one. When a group of academic psychologists asked people to name their strengths, they found that only about a third of them were actually able to say what they were, because they found it so hard to pinpoint what they were good at.

The good news is there are several ways to find out what your strengths might be.

Know what you are looking for

Your strengths are a mixture of your talents, knowledge and skills. They are a combination of qualities you were born with and those you have gained through your life experiences. They might be:

Practical strengths such as being able to build something with your hands.

Creative strengths such as being able to draw a picture, write a story or create a design.

Imaginative strengths such as being able to invent a new product or service.

Organisational strengths such as being able to organise a conference.

Problem-solving strengths such as being able to see a solution to a complex issue.

Technical or technological strengths such as being able to understand a new piece of computer software.

Communication strengths such as being able to make an inspiring speech.

People strengths such as being able to understand people's needs and to bring people together as a team.

Character strengths such as being able to be resilient when faced with repeated setbacks.

Rather than getting too bogged down in lists, however, by far the easiest way to understand what you are looking for is to ask yourself two simple questions. First, what am I good at? And, second, what do I enjoy doing? Your true strengths lie in the bit that overlaps.

Ask your friends and family

Strengths can come in all kinds of shapes and sizes. They might not be obvious, and they might not be the ones you were expecting. You might not even think that you actually have any strengths worth mentioning. Sometimes it can be hard to spot your own good qualities and to identify your positive attributes because you are so used to noticing the negatives and being critical of yourself. A good way to start looking for your strengths and attributes is to ask the people who know you well, who will be able to see the great things about you that you might not be able to.

Draw up a list of eight friends and members of your family, choosing them from different parts of your life – people you have known since you were young, people you met through work, people you see a lot and people you only see occasionally. Now send each of them the same short email, asking them to describe you in three words. Tell them not to spend too long thinking about it; ideally you want the first three words that pop into their heads.

Now study the answers. You are not especially interested in analysing individual responses; instead you are looking for trends and common themes.

Look at the words – which resonate? Which surprise you? Do any show a side of you that makes you feel surprised, or perplexed, or pleased?

When I did this myself, I found several words that I would have used to describe myself, but also words I would never have thought of using. There were other words that described traits that I thought were not obvious but that I was pleased that someone else had noticed. 'Hard-working' was an obvious one; 'independent' I was surprised at; 'quirky' I was secretly very pleased about.

One tip – if you have children in your life who know you well, whether they are your own children, or grandchildren, nieces and nephews, or children of friends, then ask them too, because they can sometimes come up with things that no one else might think to mention. From one child I got 'kind, protective and silly', and from another I got 'funny, hard-working and mad'. Both felt good.

Now think about how you might be able to use these strengths to help you achieve the goals you have identified in the previous chapters. Might some of these be useful in helping you move towards them?

Dig out your old school reports

If you are feeling brave, go round to your parents' house and spend an afternoon looking through the rotting cardboard boxes in the attic to find your old school reports. Ignore all the bits where your teachers wrote about not concentrating in class and always handing your homework in late, and focus instead on anything positive they wrote about you. At the very least it will provide you with some amusing anecdotes to tell your friends. At best, though, it might remind you of some of the good qualities you have that you had forgotten about.

You can use all these qualities and strengths to help you achieve your goals. If your teachers saw you as being diligent and tenacious, for example, how incredibly reassuring to know that you already have what it takes to stick to your plan and put the effort in to achieve your aims.

Give yourself space to think

Now that you have asked others for their input, it is time to add your own ideas about what your strengths might be. The best way to do this is to give yourself a bit of time and space to reflect on what might be your good qualities. It doesn't have to be a lot of time and space, and it doesn't have to be a formal process – a moment of quiet, or a long walk can be just as useful as an expensive retreat. Perhaps more so: my friend Mark booked himself onto a ten-day silent meditation in order to sort his thoughts out. Those on the retreat were only allowed to communicate with each other by writing notes on a piece of paper. He lasted less than 24 hours.

Whatever kind of space you manage to find, the secret is not to impose any expectations on it. You want to let your mind wander freely, not to direct its path.

Now write down what you think your strengths are. Don't be modest, because you are looking for anything that can be useful. And do make sure you write them down, because you may quickly forget the insights you've had once you go back to everyday life. A written record to refer back to is crucial. Indeed, throughout this process it can be useful to carry a notebook and pen so that you can keep all your ideas and thoughts in one place.

Now reflect on what you have written. How might these qualities be put to work to achieve your aims?

KNOWHOW

Hubud (www.hubud.org) is a co-working space in the mountain village of Ubud in Bali. It attracts people from all walks of life who want to take a break from their daily lives to explore a new idea, or a new project, or a new way of living. People can rent desk space by the day or by the month, attend courses, and stay for as long or as short as they want.

Chris Thompson, Hubud's director, says, 'The basis of Hubud is to allow people to "be themselves". We spend 20 years in education being told what to do and then many years in the working world being told what to do. This gives people the opportunity to step off that treadmill and explore things that are close to their hearts. People have the answers within themselves. They just need to find a place that allows the light to shine.'

He adds, 'People come here mostly to work or start a new idea or project. Some come to explore and find their passions. Being here allows people the opportunity to explore a different life path that has been calling to them for years. I have been hugged many times by people saying thank you for what Hubud has done for them.'

Reconfigure your negative traits

If you found the idea of identifying and writing down your strengths hard, don't worry. You are not alone. It is much easier to focus on the things that you can't do rather than the things that you can. So if you've ended up with a very short list, don't panic. Because here's the really exciting bit – you can turn even the negative character traits that you've been labelled with over the years on their head and put them to work effectively. The traits you thought you needed to ignore could actually turn out to be real assets in your quest to create a better life – all you have to do is to flip them over and look at them from the other way up. And it's important that you do this, because if you don't take action to reposition them, you could be missing out on some really useful tools.

Are you:

Impatient? Good news, this means you don't procrastinate and are good at getting things done.

Lacking in confidence? This means you are always questioning and checking rather than merely blundering on regardless.

Bossy? This means you are very much in control, a natural leader who knows what to do.

Shy? This means you are cautious, watchful and good at assessing situations before jumping in.

Impetuous? This means you are spontaneous, passionate and very driven.

Flipping your negative traits will not only make you feel more confident about what you are trying to do, it will also really help you achieve your goals, because now you have a much bigger pool of strengths to draw from.

Challenge yourself

There's another very simple way to discover where your true strengths lie. That's to take yourself out of your comfort zone and put yourself into an unfamiliar situation. Being forced to use skills that you never knew you had or to find inner resolve that you didn't know existed means that it won't take long to discover what you're really made of.

Challenging yourself can also introduce you to new interests and areas that you may never have otherwise thought of exploring.

Lisa Braund was 34 years old and feeling frustrated with her life. She had lots of ideas about what she wanted to do, but lacked confidence and was working as a temporary secretary while she tried to figure out how to take the next step. Then one day she spotted an advertisement in a newspaper asking for people to take part in a historical reality television show on Channel 4. The show, *Regency House Party*, was looking for ten single people to live in a large country house together for nine weeks, in the manner they would have done in the Regency era of the early nineteenth century. They would wear Regency clothes, eat Regency food, follow a Regency lifestyle and observe the upper-class courting rituals of the time.

The idea really appealed and so Lisa applied to be on the show. She says, 'I wanted a change and this was like being given a chance to live a different life.'

She was chosen to take part and a few months later was on her way in a horse-drawn carriage to a stately home in Herefordshire, wearing a bonnet and corset with an Empire line long dress. However, Lisa quickly discovered it was not all dressing up and parties. Living as though they were in Regency times meant chamber pots under the beds instead of toilets, having only one bath a week, and doing without toothpaste, deodorant, razors and shampoo. The only contact she had with the outside world was by writing letters with quill pen and ink.

Worse still, as a single woman Lisa had to be constantly accompanied by an older female chaperone and was not allowed to talk to the men without an introduction. It was often frustrating, particularly as the women had to stay behind in the house reading and sewing while the men went off hunting and shooting.

But Lisa not only survived the experience, she thrived on it, throwing herself into every challenge that came her way. At the end of the show, the viewers voted her the most popular girl. By the time she left she was far more confident about her own qualities and skills, such as her ability to get on with all kinds of people, and to cope with uncomfortable physical situations. She had also discovered a whole new area of work that she really enjoyed.

She says, 'I surprised myself. To start with it was all really difficult, but I adapted and realised I had options I hadn't even thought about. It was life-changing.'

After the show Lisa decided that she wanted to work in television herself and so got a job with Endemol, the production company, before becoming a researcher for the BAFTAs, the UK's annual film and television awards. She now works for FOS, a film and television production company.

KNOWHOW

If you like the idea of putting yourself in a challenging physical environment, the Youth Hostel Association (www.yha.org.uk) runs activity courses such as canoeing and caving at its hostels in Edale and Okehampton.

If you have a bigger budget, check out adventure holiday companies such as Exodus (www.exodus.co.uk) and Explore (www.explore.co.uk). Trekking to Everest Base Camp for 17 days is likely to reveal sides of you that you had no idea about.

If you fancy challenging yourself in a completely different way, you could apply to take part in a television show. Do you like the idea of being a contestant on *The Voice*? Then visit the ITV website (www.itv.com/beontv). Or how about taking part in *The Island with Bear Grylls*? In that case it's Channel 4 (www.channel4.com/programmes/take-part).

Discover your transferable skills

Transferable skills are ones you learn while doing one thing that you can then easily use to do something else completely different.

Recruitment specialists and careers advisors get extremely excited about the idea of transferable skills, because instead of being limited to seeking one specific sort of job, candidates with transferable skills have the ability to work in lots of different industries in many different kinds of roles, dramatically expanding the number of positions they can apply for.

According to Reed, the recruitment firm, the most important transferable skills are leadership, motivation, time management, prioritisation, delegation, listening, communication, analytics and research. You could usefully use all of these in almost any kind of situation, market or industry.

If you look a little closer at the skills you already possess, you may find that many of them are applicable to several different situations and can be used in more ways than you think.

KNOWHOW

For a more detailed list of transferable skills, check out The Steps to Work website (www.stepstowork.co.uk) – just click on their Get Ready to Find Work link under the Looking for a Job section.

Become a volunteer

You can find out a huge amount about yourself and the skills you already have by becoming a volunteer. That might mean helping out in your local hospice once a week, or working at a local National Trust property, or listening to children read in primary schools.

Volunteering is not just a good way to find out what you are good at, it can also be a useful way to find out what you are hopeless at. I once answered an advert asking for volunteers to work on an archaeological dig in the Outer Hebrides. I thought it might be fun. But after two weeks of being cold, wet, wind-blasted and miserable, I realised I never wanted to have a job that involved working outside, or that required hard physical work, and that I wasn't in the slightest bit interested in archaeology. A pretty useful two weeks, I think you'll agree.

There are other benefits to volunteering too. It has been proven that volunteering doesn't just enhance your skills, it can also improve your job prospects. A recent survey by Deloitte found that firms place a huge importance on candidates who have volunteer experience, with 92 per cent saying that volunteering improves employees' leadership skills and 82 per cent saying they were more likely to choose a candidate with volunteer experience on their CV.

KNOWHOW

To find volunteering opportunities in your area, check out the National Council for Voluntary Organisations website (www.ncvo.org.uk) or the Volunteers Week website (www.volunteers.org) and click on 'I want to volunteer'. You can search by postcode. You can also follow Volunteers Week on Twitter @NCVOVolunteers. Alternatively, consider volunteering for the Citizen's Advice Bureau (www.citizensadvice.org.uk), a nationwide organisation that provides people with free advice to overcome their problems; or the Samaritans (www.samaritans.org), a telephone helpline service that helps people who are struggling to cope or who are at risk of suicide.

Boost your best bits

If you assess your strengths and attributes and realise there are some big gaps, don't panic. The good news is you don't have to be good at everything. You just have to start using the bits you are good at to maximum effect.

After all, even the actual superheroes aren't good at everything. Superman is great at flying and getting changed very fast in phone boxes, but really doesn't cope well with kryptonite. Batman is fantastic at fighting villains, but hopeless at forming relationships. Wonder Woman is extremely strong, but goes into an uncontrollable rage if her bracelets get lost or broken. And Spiderman is brilliant at making spiders' webs, but terrible at making decisions. If you happened to catch any of them on a bad day, at the wrong moment in the wrong situation, they would be useless at saving the world.

Just like the superheroes, you can supercharge your best qualities and strengths. It will more than make up for your deficiencies in other areas.

Put the effort in

First, the bad news. Success doesn't just show up without effort. No matter how many 'get-rich-quick' schemes might wish to persuade you otherwise, you have to put the work in, or it's just not going to happen. Annoying but true. Every successful person I have ever met works really hard at what they do. And so must you.

The idea of working hard to achieve success is not a message that everyone wants to hear. It sounds far more whizz-bang exciting to cut to the last frame of the movie, which shows you sitting on your yacht sipping champagne. Yet putting in the effort can supercharge your talent and skills like nothing else can.

Jeffrey Archer was a Conservative MP, but when he became a casualty of a fraudulent investment scheme, he faced the prospect of going bankrupt so had to stand down from his parliamentary seat and sell the family home. By then aged 34, he decided to try writing novels to restore his fortunes.

His first book, *Not a Penny More, Not a Penny Less*, took him nine months to write and was initially rejected by 17 publishers. However the eighteenth publisher agreed to publish it, paying him a modest advance of £3,000. He followed that with another book, *Shall We Tell the President?*, for which he got an advance of £8,000.

His decision to write for a living really paid off however when his third novel, *Kane and Abel*, landed a US $3.2 million advance, following a bidding war among US publishers. He says, 'It changed my life overnight.'

Jeffrey has now written more than 25 books and sold 277 million copies worldwide, earning him an estimated £54 million fortune. *Kane and Abel* alone has sold more than 34 million copies and is one of the most successful books ever published.

But all these books have not come about by accident. For each book Jeffrey follows the same strict writing routine. He gets up at 5.30am and writes for eight hours a day in four blocks of two hours, going for long walks in between each writing session, and going to bed at 10pm.

He follows this routine every day for six weeks, then takes four weeks off before beginning work again following the same routine. Each book takes him around a year to research and a year to write. It typically takes him six weeks to do the first draft, writing it in longhand with a pen and paper, but he will then revise it several times, often producing 14 drafts before submitting it for publication.

In 2009 he even spent nine months rewriting his bestseller *Kane and Abel*, in the process cutting 40,000 original words and adding 27,000 new ones, because he felt it would be a better book if it was leaner and more fast-paced.

Jeffrey says that putting in the effort has been key to his success as a novelist. He says, 'I am a hard worker. I am ruthless. By working hard you become a better craftsman and more capable at your job. Now when I sit down to write, I try to remember all the mistakes I have made over the past 30 years and I know the way to do things.'

Indeed he believes that hard work is as important as talent to achieve success in any field. 'You can still survive without the talent, but you can't survive without the hard work. If you have a talent and don't work, you won't get anywhere.'

Keep learning

Successful people place huge importance on continually learning new things, no matter what field they are in. They attend courses and conferences, they read widely, they consult experts, they employ coaches. Some of them in business have even introduced reverse mentoring programmes, in which the more senior people in a company spend time learning about the world from younger, more junior employees, who can often provide them with fresh insight into fast-changing areas such as new technology and social media.

There's a good reason for this emphasis on learning. As

well as being interesting in itself, learning something new can spark off all kinds of thoughts and ideas that you weren't expecting. Most importantly, continual learning is a fantastic way to keep improving and sharpening your best qualities to ensure they are the very best they can be at all times.

KNOWHOW

There are plenty of opportunities for you to keep on learning. How about watching some TED talks at www.ted.com/talks – there are more than 2,400 of them available to watch online, covering hundreds of topics from science and entertainment to business and global issues? Just click on one you like the look of and start watching; they are all free.

The Open University (www.open.ac.uk) offers more than 1,000 free online courses in all kind of subjects from philosophy to Spanish. You can start a course whenever you want and complete it in your own time.

Or visit the Floodlight website (www.floodlight. co.uk). Formerly a guide to courses solely in London, the website is now nationwide and has a database of more than 100,000 part-time and online courses in every possible subject.

The School of Life (www.theschooloflife.com) in London was set up to provide people with good ideas for everyday life and it now runs classes, courses, events and workshops about practical issues such as how to find fulfilling work, how to make relationships work and how to achieve calm in your life.

Keep at it

Playing to your strengths does not just mean finding them and shouting hooray. You need to flex those strengths regularly to keep them working as they should, and so that they become even stronger and even more useful.

It's a bit like playing scales on the piano. The more you do it, the better you get. And if you can get into a regular routine of doing it, the rewards will multiply. Never underestimate the power of little and often, and of just plugging away at something.

Elizabeth Gilbert is the author of the bestselling book *Eat Pray Love*, which tells her personal story of going on a journey of self-discovery to Italy, India and Bali after her marriage broke down. The book has been an incredible success, selling 10 million copies worldwide in 30 languages, and was made into a film starring Julia Roberts.

But before she achieved such enormous success with *Eat Pray Love*, Elizabeth struggled for many years to find a publisher for the books she wrote. She says that for her the answer was to simply keep on writing.

In a TED talk she says, 'Let the records show that I showed up for my part of the job. Don't be afraid, don't be daunted, just do your job, continue to show up for your piece of it, whatever that might be. If your job is to dance, do your dance. Olé to you just for having the sheer human love and stubbornness to keep showing up.'

You too need to have the love and stubbornness to keep showing up, even on those days when it feels as though you are not making any progress. It is only by keeping at it that you give your strengths the best possible chance to shine through.

NOW TAKE ACTION

1. Describe yourself in three words, using only positive descriptions.

2. Analyse how you spend your time. Are there particular tasks and activities that you enjoy doing more than others, either at work or at home?

3. Think about how you might challenge yourself to see what you are made of. How about climbing a mountain, entering a competition, applying to be a contestant on a television show or going on an expedition?

———

Chapter 4

Decide how you work best

*'People rarely succeed at anything
unless they have fun doing it'*

Dale Carnegie, writer

N ot that long ago there was pretty much only one way of working – you got a job and you went to your place of work, typically from 9am to 5pm each day, five days a week, and had four weeks holiday each year.

But big advances in technology and communication have changed all that. Depending on what type of work you choose to do, and which industry you work in, there are now dozens of ways of working. You have the option of working from home, or of working remotely from other locations or while on the move, of working longer hours, or shorter hours, of working on specific projects and taking time off in between, or any combination of the above.

And the options are continually expanding. The UK Government has introduced new legislation that gives employees the right to request flexible working arrangements from their employers; meanwhile there is a growing number of people who describe themselves as digital nomads and work from remote corners of the world with nothing but a smartphone and a laptop.

All of which means that you have a lot more freedom to choose the way you want to work. So now that you have identified your strengths, you can structure the way you work in order to make the most of them.

You have three main options:

1. Be an employee working for someone else

This means you typically work for one employer doing one kind of role. You are likely to receive a regular fixed wage or salary and work set hours, and you may have the opportunity to pursue a defined career path. The big advantage of this route is the security of a regular salary, and the possibility of a structured career progression.

2. Work for yourself

You can do this either as a self-employed freelancer or by starting your own business. Either way, you will typically work for several clients at a time and may do a variety of different roles. You get paid only if you actually have work to do, your working hours might be irregular and there is no defined career path – however, you do get the chance to create one of your own.

3. Do a mixture of both

Big advances in technology, combined with greater flexibility in the workplace, means that, in a growing number of professions, it is now possible to combine salaried work with working for yourself. That might mean holding down a full-time time job during the day, while starting up and running your own business in the evenings and at weekends. Or it might mean having a part-time job and leaving the rest of your working week free to pursue your own freelance projects. The advantage of this hybrid model is that it gives you the security of a regular income – you know the mortgage or rent and the bills will be paid each month – while still leaving you free to pursue your own goals and projects that really get your pulse racing.

Any of these three options can potentially take you where you want to be – the secret is to choose the one that plays best to your strengths. So let's take a look at each of them in turn:

The employee option

Here are the key strengths you need to develop to make this work well:

• Reliability

At the very least an employer needs to know that you are going to show up on time, every day, and get the job done. The company that employs you will also want to know that you are not going to storm out and threaten to resign every time something doesn't go your way.

• Leadership and management skills

As you progress through an organisation you are likely to be required to lead and manage other people. You will need to inspire them, guide them and monitor their progress in an effective way to make the most of the skills they have to offer. This requires patience, confidence and understanding.

● The ability to work well as part of a team

Working within an organisation is all about working together with other people. Doing this well requires you to be assertive where needed, be able to compromise where required, and have strong interpersonal skills to enable you to get on with people, even if you have very little in common and see the world in a different way.

● Communication skills

When you are working with other people on a daily basis, it is important to be able to get your message across, whether that is speaking up in a meeting or making yourself heard at a team bonding session.

● Adaptability

As you rise through an organisation, the nature of your job is likely to change and you may be given new tasks and responsibilities. Indeed the nature of the business itself may change as it reacts to changes in its markets. Sometimes you may be taken off a project you were working on, and moved elsewhere within the organisation. Or you may be given work you don't really want to do. You need to be flexible enough to take these changes in your stride and make the best of them, without complaint.

● The ability to stay calm

Sometimes other people may take credit for your ideas or achievements, or sideline you from projects you initiated. Or you may find that your superiors reject your proposals for new ways of doing things or new projects. As an employee you need to be able to stay calm, to accept compromise, and to conduct yourself well through these and any other difficult situations.

The self-employed option

These are the key strengths that you need to develop in order to make a success of working for yourself:

• Self-discipline

Being self-employed comes with a lot of freedom and independence. Depending on what type of work you are doing, you may be able to choose when and where you work, when you start and stop each day, and how much time you take off for other activities. If you're doing some work for someone, your client won't care whether you work on their project at the kitchen table, at a desk in your spare bedroom or in a local cafe, and whether you are working between the hours of 9am and 5pm or between 10pm and 3am – as long as you deliver their project to them on time and to their required standard. Using this freedom well requires a strong sense of discipline. If you think you are more likely to spend your days meeting friends for coffee or getting distracted by household tasks, then self-employment may not be for you.

• Self-motivation

Work isn't just going to show up on your doorstep – you are going to have to go out and find it, again and again. That may mean sending emails, writing proposals, doing pitches, attending conferences and networking constantly, even when you don't feel like it. Being self-employed means taking full responsibility for creating an income for yourself and ensuring that you have enough work coming in.

• Good organisational skills

As well as doing the work itself, being self-employed comes with a surprising amount of admin. You constantly need to send and chase invoices, calculate expenses, do tax and VAT returns, get any permits you need, sort out services such as broadband and mobile phones, and make your own hotel and transport arrangements for any events you attend. You need to put in place good systems for doing all this otherwise you will quickly get overwhelmed. If you are doing a variety of different projects, you will also need to be really organised to ensure that everything stays on track. This may mean keeping notes, making files, staying on top of deadlines and keeping clients up to date.

• Knowledge

As a self-employed person you will need to have a good understanding of how your industry works, so that you can see where the work is likely to come from, how to access it and who is likely to give it to you. This means that you will need to either have a great deal of knowledge about the industry you are operating in, or be willing to learn, fast.

• Self-determination

When you are self-employed there is no fixed career path to follow. This is potentially very exciting as it means you can steer your career in the direction you want, by deliberately pitching for certain kinds of work you enjoy doing and creating a public profile – through your website and social media accounts – that reflects the kind of work you want to do. It also means that you can try out several different types of role at once – perhaps doing a writing project for one client, an organising project for another, and a design project for a third. You are also free to explore different ways of working, from partnerships to collaboration with others, from communal collectives to co-operatives. All of this is very exciting and liberating, but you are the one who needs to make things happen.

• Resilience

Being self-employed is an unpredictable way to earn a living. There may be days or even weeks when you don't have enough – or even any – work to do, and other times when you have far too much of it. It can also be impossible to judge the amount of work coming your way, or when it is going to show up, which makes it difficult to plan ahead or to manage your workflow. For this reason it can also be hard to take time off for holidays and social events. I once had to interrupt a holiday in France for a one-hour meeting in London that had been moved at the last minute. I got into the car, drove to London for the meeting and then drove straight back to France again. The more you can embrace the unexpected bumps in the ride, the happier you will be. And the more resilient and flexible you show your clients you are, the more repeat business you are likely to get.

The hybrid option

To be both an employee and self-employed requires the following strengths:

• Focus

When you have several different jobs or projects on the go at the same time, you need to be totally focused on the task in front of you and to stop thinking about all the tasks that need to be done at another time. With so much potential for distraction, it is important to ensure that everything you do has your full attention at that moment.

• Discipline

Sometimes when one role or project is going particularly well, or is going through a really exciting stage, you are going to want to do that role or project all the time. But you need to be really disciplined about giving the right amount of time and energy to all your projects. Don't jeopardise your employed role because something has suddenly become really interesting in your freelance life; and don't jeopardise your own business by becoming too engrossed in a project relating to your salaried role.

• The ability to set realistic expectations

Because you are dividing your time between two or more different roles, you may not be able to progress either one as quickly as you would if you were focusing on one of them full time. Be patient and keep in mind the benefits of why you are working this way.

• Good time-management skills

When you are juggling two – or more – working lives, you don't have time to fritter away precious hours. You need to make every moment count.

Here's an example of how this hybrid model can work brilliantly. Janan Leo knew she wanted to set up her own business after discovering that there was a gap in the market for foldable flat shoes that women could wear while commuting to work, but that were small enough for them to store in a handbag when they arrived at work and changed out of them.

She was able to start her business, Cocorose London, with £3,000 of savings and create a concept and prototype for her shoes. But with the business still in start-up mode, Janan needed to support herself and the business financially by remaining in employment too. So, she continued to work full time as New Product Development Manager for Virgin Trains, while she focused on developing Cocorose London in her spare time before and after work and at weekends.

She says, 'This was before the days of social media, so I would get up early to hand out flyers at Tube stations before going to work each day. On Saturdays I would fold the shoes into their little travel purses so that on Sundays I could sell them on a market stall in East London. I was constantly thinking how I could use my time wisely while not at work.'

Janan also started selling her shoes via her website, www.cocoroselondon.com.

It was immensely hard work juggling the two roles and she didn't get much sleep. But by starting her business in her spare time, Janan considerably reduced the financial risk of going it alone and kept her options open if her business did not work out.

She says, 'It was hard work, but it made me feel less anxious, knowing that I could support myself and pay my own bills. I wouldn't have been able to set up the business without having that financial support. I know that it made my parents feel better too. In a strange way it also really helped me to focus, because I knew I had only limited time to work on the business.'

After three years her business was doing well enough to

pay Janan a salary, so she was able to take redundancy from her day job with Virgin and work on it full time. Cocorose London has now sold hundreds of thousands of pairs of shoes around the world via its website and through independent boutiques and department stores.

NOW TAKE ACTION

1. Think about whether your expertise lends itself to self-employment. Could you continue doing the same kind of work as you do now, or would you have to radically change direction? Would you want to?

2. Are you the type of person who can self-motivate? Do you like working independently? Does the social side of an office environment appeal to you or leave you cold?

3. Look at the ways in which you already successfully juggle different aspects of your life – such as work, family, chores, socialising and exercise. Does the juggling feel overwhelming or rewarding?

———————

Chapter 5

Don't let anything hold you back

'Obstacles don't have to stop you. If you run into a wall, don't turn around and give up. Figure out how to climb it, go through it, or work around it'

Michael Jordan, basketball player

Having discovered your direction, your strengths and the way you'd like to work, it's time to look at what could stand in the way of making your plans a reality.

There is a lovely song that is often sung to babies and toddlers at playgroups and nurseries. It goes something like this: 'Zoom zoom zoom, we're going to the moon. Zoom zoom zoom, we'll be there very soon. Five, four, three, two, one, blast off!'

What is so great about the song, apart from its sheer sense of fun and adventure, is the simple calm confidence that because we've decided to go to the moon, that is what is going to happen. No mention of any difficulties or obstacles that might stand in our way, or concerns about something going wrong, or doubts we might not make it. No discussion about whether we are crazy to think of attempting such a thing, or what other people might think. Instead the song simply announces that we are off to the moon, that we will be there very soon, and that's that.

It's a fantastic approach to life. If you start out with the idea that nothing is going to hold you back, then you are more likely to be right, because you will be determined to find a way around every obstacle in your path, no matter how challenging each obstacle may be.

Unfortunately it can be easy to feel overwhelmed by all the potential hurdles in the way, both real and imagined. For example, you might think you are too old, too young, too inexperienced, too poor, too busy, too shy, too unfit or too disorganised to be a success in life. Instead of seeing all the advantages and assets you possess, all you can see are the drawbacks.

But obstacles – whether real or imagined – are only obstacles if you let them be. The secret is to turn every potential obstacle on its head, so that all those negatives become positives, and anything that you think is blocking your progress becomes an opportunity to help rather than hinder you. It's a similar approach to dealing with your negative character traits. Let's look at how this can work in practice:

Think you are too old? Good news: success is not age dependent. Your age means you have accumulated lots of experience, skills and knowledge about how the world works, all of which are going to come in very handy.

Think you lack knowledge and experience? That's fine: you have no preconceived ideas about how to do things and so are free to create your own path, while at the same time being open-minded enough to listen to and heed sound advice from others when or if you need it.

Think your family commitments will get in the way? Not only can raising children make you really good at using your time efficiently and productively, your kids can also fire up your imagination like nothing else can. Family life can provide you with all the motivation and inspiration you need.

Think your personal circumstances will hold you back? Good news: you don't have to let them define you, or even describe you, and they might ultimately prove to be a help not a hindrance.

Worried about a lack of money? A lack of cash may initially feel like a drawback, but it could force you to think more creatively about how you tackle a project, which could eventually turn out to be an advantage.

Let's take a look at some of the obstacles you might encounter.

Lack of knowledge or experience

There is nothing more crushing than announcing to friends that you are going to do something amazing, and then seeing them look at you with a mixture of pity and amusement in their eyes. Or listening to them say, 'But what do you know about that?' Knowledge and experience can be immensely useful, but they don't have to be a deal breaker. You can still get on just fine without them, as long as you are prepared to learn as you go along.

Fraser Doherty was just 14 when he started making jam from a recipe his grandmother had taught him. He discovered he could make a healthier version of the jam by using apple juice instead of sugar and was soon selling it door to door near his home in Edinburgh.

When he was 16 Fraser decided that he'd like to sell his jam in supermarkets. He didn't know how to go about doing this, however, so he went along to one of Waitrose's Meet the Buyers days to get some advice. Waitrose loved his jam, but said that he needed to go and find a factory that could make it for him. Fraser didn't know how to do this either but, undaunted, he simply contacted factories and showed them his jam until one of them agreed to take him on. He went back to tell Waitrose, but they told him he needed to sort out some branding and packaging too. Fraser also had no idea how to do this, but he began to think about a new name for his jam and a design for his label, and after much trial and error he renamed his jam 'SuperJam'. Eventually, a year later, Waitrose agreed to stock it.

His business now sells up to one million jars of SuperJam every year in more than a thousand supermarkets around the world. It has also unexpectedly become one of the biggest-selling jams in South Korea. Fraser also holds SuperJam tea dances throughout the UK for retired people, who get together for afternoon tea, dancing and nostalgia.

Fraser is now 28 and has been awarded an MBE for services to business. He says, 'I didn't have any money and I didn't know anything about supermarkets or factories. I had to figure it all out. But I was always honest about the fact that I didn't have any experience and when I told people that I didn't really know how to do something and please could they point me in the right direction, they would usually give me advice and be happy to help. The best thing you can do is to show how passionate you are about something and show that you take it seriously.'

> **KNOWHOW**
>
> If you need to know how to do something specific, check out wikiHow (www.wikihow.com). The website has hundreds of free 'how to' articles on all kinds of subjects.

You don't know the right people

Of course it would be great to have a network of useful contacts to call upon, but if you don't know anyone who might be able to help you with your venture, the good news is it doesn't matter because you can still do brilliantly on your own.

When Wendy Shand was on holiday with her family in France, her two-year-old son fell into an unguarded pool. Fortunately, her father noticed and jumped in to rescue him, but it got Wendy thinking about how she could make holidays safer for other families with young children. She decided to start a business offering holiday villas for families that would come equipped with everything needed to keep babies and toddlers safe on holiday, from stairgates, cots and high chairs to enclosed pools. Because families with young children can travel outside the peak season school holidays, she hoped that villa owners might see the benefits of being more likely to rent out their properties at other times of the year and agree to buy the equipment they needed.

It was a bold plan. Wendy was a full-time mother of three young children living in a remote corner of Wales and had never even worked in the travel industry, let alone started a business in it. However, she got in touch with a few holiday home owners in France and offered to market their properties on her website in return for a commission on any holidays booked.

Nine owners agreed to give it a go, so Wendy created a simple website featuring their properties. Then in April 2006 she wrote a press release announcing the launch of her business, and sent it out to a handful of business journalists.

One of those journalists was me. I was the Enterprise Editor of *The Sunday Times* and I happened to be writing a feature about Internet start-ups. I loved Wendy's business idea and rang her for a chat. I included a paragraph about her fledgling business in my feature, which ran the following Sunday under the headline 'Online start-ups return to a place in the sun'. It was accompanied by a large photo of Wendy and two of her children, taken on the beach by her house.

The impact was instant. Wendy was immediately flooded with interest from readers keen to book a holiday and her business took off. She says now that the *Sunday Times* piece, together with a smaller one in *The Times* the following day, prompted so many calls from potential customers that her business made £25,000 worth of commission in its first season, getting it off to a great start.

Her business Tots to Travel (www.totstotravel.com) has continued to grow and now has a turnover of £10 million and 30 staff. More than 5,000 families book holidays with her each year. Tots to Travel now also offers holidays for pre-school families in their own branded and equipped villas at overseas resorts.

Wendy, who has recruited her husband Rob to help her run the business, says, 'At the beginning I had no idea whether my business would work or not, but I knew I had nothing to lose by trying. I am incredibly proud of what we have achieved so far.'

KNOWHOW

You can write your own press release using a free template from the internet and email it to specific journalists yourself. Alternatively, a press distribution service such as Pressat (www.pressat.co.uk) will send a single press release on your behalf to lots of journalists for a one-off fee.

Your age

Our society is obsessed with how old people are, and what they think this means they can and can't do. This is taken to its extremes in tabloid newspapers such as the *Daily Mail*, which constantly runs features analysing how good or bad people look for their age. But just because other people endlessly go on about age doesn't mean that you have to. Being old, or indeed young, has nothing to do with your ability to achieve great things. Only your attitude towards age does.

Mary Wesley wrote her first children's book when she was 57 and her first adult novel at the age of 71. Colonel Sanders was in his sixties when he developed his Kentucky Fried Chicken franchise. Even Ricky Gervais had already turned 40 when the BBC broadcast his first television series, *The Office*. On the other hand Nick D'Aloisio sold his first business, Summly, at the age of 17 for US \$30 million.

A study of nearly 3,000 physicists from 1893 onwards found that the point at which they achieved breakthrough success in their field had nothing to do with how young or old they were. Rather, the survey, led by Dr Roberta Sinatra at the Central European University in Budapest, found that the physicists' most successful work was randomly scattered throughout their lives. Age just wasn't a significant factor – what counted far more was how productive they were in the number of papers they published.

Changes in employment legislation mean companies are no longer able to force people to automatically leave their job when they hit retirement age. Provided you are still physically and mentally able to do your job, you can go on for as long as you want. You can retrain to become a lawyer, or a teacher or a nurse, in your forties, fifties and beyond, and there is no upper age limit to studying at university as a mature student. The University Advice service UCAS (www.ucas.com) has a dedicated section for those wanting to return to study later in life.

KNOWHOW

Start listening to how you talk. Many people start labelling themselves as old long before they need to. Don't be one of them. If you ever catch yourself telling people how old you are when they haven't even asked, or using the words 'young people these days' or 'at my age', then stop, right now. Instead follow Diana Athill's lead. She worked for the publishing house André Deutsch for many years and began writing books of her own when she was 45. Her latest memoir, *Alive, Alive Oh!*, was published when she was 98. In it she describes one of the people living in her retirement home as 'quite young (only in her mid-eighties)'. Priceless.

You have a young family

Raising a family can give you two potential obstacles to overcome. First, there is the fear that the effort needed to bring them up will sap your energy and vitality and leave you too worn out and uninspired to achieve amazing things. And, second, there is the sheer practical challenge of trying to look after children while also pursuing a career or project.

The good news is that neither needs to stand in your way. Let's look at them in turn:

1. Inspiration

The first one is easily dealt with. The literary critic Cyril Connolly wrote, 'There is no more sombre enemy of good art than the pram in the hall.' He was suggesting that the moment you had children you could wave goodbye to any chance of achieving brilliant creative endeavour. But he was talking nonsense. Although he had two children of his own, it wasn't his children who stopped him becoming the great novelist that he dreamed of becoming. It was all the other distractions he allowed into his life, such as travel, politics, socialising, journalism and day-dreaming, that stopped him – plus the fact that he simply didn't have the talent he hoped he might have.

Having young children does not have to stop you achieving more – on the contrary your kids may even provide the inspiration, focus and motivation for your goal.

Jayne Hynes felt it was important to try to give her two young daughters healthy home-cooked food as often as possible, even though she was working full time as a chartered surveyor. So every weekend she would make several large batches of meals and freeze them. Her kids loved them – and when their friends came round for tea, so did they.

Inspired by her children's response, Jayne wondered if there might be a gap in the market for her frozen meals.

After researching her target market by talking to local parents and testing which of her meals children liked best, Jayne gave up her job and launched her business Kiddyum in 2015, funded with £150,000 raised from private investors. She now sells hundreds of thousands of her meals a year in Sainsbury's supermarkets and through Ocado.

Jayne says she would never have set up her own business if it hadn't been for her children. 'I just wouldn't have known that there was a gap in the market, because I wouldn't have been looking for it. My business was 100 per cent inspired by my children.'

Not only that, but her children have given meaning and purpose to what she does. She says, 'Chartered surveying was a job, but this is a passion.'

2. Logistics

No one has yet to satisfactorily resolve the dilemma of how to make four weeks of annual leave stretch to cover the 13 or more weeks of school holidays that children have each year. But the good news is that recent changes in legislation mean that anyone who has worked for the same employer for more than six months has the right to ask if they can work flexibly. That could mean starting and finishing work earlier or later than the typical nine-to-five day, or it could mean working from home part or all of the time, or working a full-time week in terms of hours, but over fewer days. It might even mean job sharing. Whatever the arrangement,

---

KNOWHOW

One unexpected benefit of having young children is that they can introduce you to interesting people. The most effective networking opportunity is not at the private members' club or the gym, the industry networking event or the office canteen – it's at the school gate or on the playing field at your children's primary school. Sporting events in particular are the ideal opportunity to meet new people in an informal way, because you are all there on an equal footing and none of you can leave until the final whistle is blown. And you never know who might show up and be able to help you with your idea. Sadly, this networking opportunity disappears when your children move up to secondary school and no longer want you to cheer them on, so make the most of it while you can.

---

there are more ways to make it easier to fit your work around family, so that you are better able to juggle raising children with doing your job, than ever before.

Of course, your employer has the right to refuse your request for flexible working, but firms are beginning to realise that such arrangements can benefit them too. For example, they can increase productivity and improve loyalty among members of their workforce. In a survey of 1,051 employees by the Chartered Institute of Personnel and Development, 54 per cent of subjects said that flexible working enabled them to have a better work/life balance, while 28 per cent said that it had been a factor in them staying with their current employer, and 25 per cent said it helped them to be more productive at work.

You can find out more about flexible working at Gov.uk (www.gov.uk), or check out the information on the Acas website (www.acas.org.uk).

Money

It's so tempting to blame a lack of money for not being able to do the things you want to do, and not being the person you want to be. And yes, of course, it would be nice to be able to throw money at goals, to help achieve them faster or with less effort. But a lack of money does not have to mean a lack of achievement. Money isn't the key to your success – you are.

This means you have a straight choice. You can either spend your days endlessly dreaming about winning the lottery, or you can get on with achieving your goals anyway – with the mortgage, overdraft and bank loan accompanying you on your way.

Here are some thoughts on how to do this.

1. Get to grips with your finances

First, you need to know what you are dealing with. Set aside an evening to go through your finances with a calculator. How much money comes in each month? How much goes out? Where does it go? Which costs are fixed, and which are variable? Which are essential and which are discretionary? The more you understand how the money flows around your life, the more in control you will be. The website MoneySavingExpert (www.moneysavingexpert.com) has several free tools and calculators, including a Savings calculator, an Income Tax calculator and a money-saving IQ test.

2. Think creatively

Sometimes a lack of money can really get the creative juices flowing. My mother loves buying and selling antiques. But because she does not have much money to invest, she cannot simply buy the popular big-ticket items and sell them on for a profit. Instead, she has to be a lot more meticulous and rigorous, spending hours researching her specialist areas carefully so she knows exactly what to look out for and what special marks and labels to identify, before trawling through car boot sales and junk shops to find the hidden treasures that other people overlook. Her approach is a lot more demanding and time-consuming, but when she does come across something special, it is also much more exciting and rewarding.

Not long ago she bought a small wooden sculpture from a junk shop for £2.50, thinking that its curious shape and pencil signature on the bottom might be significant. They were. A research session on Google revealed that the sculpture was by a highly respected artist, and that a dealer in his work lived close by. My mother got in touch to see if he would be interested in what she had found. He was. The next day she sold him the sculpture for £220, making herself a profit of £217.50 – an 8,700-per-cent return on her initial £2.50 investment.

3. Take advantage of free technology

Advances in technology have given you an incredible opportunity to do things for free that would have cost a fortune just a few years ago. You can set up websites, contact anyone via email, make Internet phone calls to anywhere in the world – all for free. And that's just the start. If you want to hold an event and invite people to it, you can do so for free using Eventbrite (www.eventbrite.com). Or you can send a newsletter to a large group of people for free with MailChimp (www.mailchimp.com). There are dozens of other such applications on the Internet that can help you, many of them either free or low cost.

4. Use your assets more effectively

Even if you don't have much ready cash available, you may be able to trade your assets and skills for the things you want to do. If you'd like to go and live abroad or in a different area for a while in order to work or study, for example, or simply to try something new, it doesn't have to cost a fortune. Instead of having to find the money to rent somewhere overseas, you could do a house swap with someone who is looking to live where you do. Neither of you will pay any rent so, apart from a small administrative fee, the arrangement will cost you nothing. Check out Home Exchange (www.homeexchange.com), or Guardian Home Exchange (www.guardianhomeexchange.co.uk). Or, if you are good with animals you could pet-sit, in an arrangement whereby you look after someone's house and pets in exchange for free accommodation while they are away. Try Housesitters (www.housesitters.co.uk) or Trusted House Sitters (www. trustedhousesitters.com).

Alternatively, you could use your language skills to teach English as a foreign language and in doing so fund a stay overseas. Take an accredited, internationally recognised qualification at TEFL (www.tefl.com) or I to I (www.i-to-i.com). Or you could use your strengths to become a volunteer with VSO (vso.org.uk), the international development organisation that helps fight poverty in developing countries.

You could even use your practical skills to start a completely new life for very little money. Julia Pyke and Gareth Shone used to live in Berkshire, where she was a hairdresser and he worked as a cobbler. But they dreamed of becoming self-sufficient and exploring a different way to live. So they bought a run-down farmhouse in rural Hungary for £3,000 that they found on the property website Rightmove (www.rightmove.co.uk). The house itself was in pretty poor shape, falling down in parts and with no electricity and only an outside tap. But it also came with lots of land where they could raise chickens and grow vegetables.

They are now on their way to becoming self-sufficient, able to live on just £6 a day. Despite having to overcome obstacles, such as learning Hungarian, they are clearly having the time of their lives. When television presenter Ben Fogle came to film them for his Channel 5 show *New Lives in the Wild*, Julia told him, 'I like not knowing what tomorrow holds and what challenges we will have. I have found the less you have, the better off you are, as you can focus on who you are and what you want from life.'

5. Earn while you learn

Becoming an apprentice can be a handy route into a new career because you study on the job, typically attending college one day a week. You will be paid the national minimum wage and be taught job-specific skills. The apprenticeship scheme has recently been extended in the UK and is now available for more than 1,500 roles in 170 industries. Apprenticeships now also provide qualifications that are equivalent to academic qualifications – an Advanced Level-3 apprenticeship, for example, is equivalent to two A Levels. You can find out more at the Government information service Gov.uk (www.gov.uk) – just type in the word apprenticeships.

Internships are another way to gain practical experience while you work, especially now that there has been a clampdown on unpaid internships. Several organisations have been set up to provide people with a way into internships – check out www.gov.uk/find-internship and also Inspiring Interns (www.inspiringinterns.com) and Enternships (www.enternships.com).

6. Get crowdfunding

If you really can't get your project off the ground without some cash, you may be able to raise the money you need using crowdfunding. This enables you to pitch your idea to hundreds of individual investors who can invest small amounts in projects they like the look of. That means that you could raise hundreds or even thousands of pounds to fund your cookbook, art exhibition or canoeing expedition, simply by posting up some details on a crowdfunding website. Kickstarter (www.kickstarter.com) and Indiegogo (www.indiegogo.com) in particular have been set up to fund creative projects; check them out.

In 2016 a group of people decided to replace all the adverts in Clapham Common Underground station with pictures of cats for two weeks, to highlight the value of friends and experiences over material possessions. They raised £23,000 via crowdfunding to pay for it and teamed up with two cat charities, Battersea Dogs & Cats home and Cats Protection, to include pictures of real stray cats in need of homes.

The campaign attracted a huge amount of positive publicity from newspapers and television stations around the world, with many people loving the craziness of what the group had achieved. In a blog post explaining the campaign, one of the organisers, James Turner, said, 'This project has uncorked a kind of energy that I haven't experienced before. We want to inspire people to think differently about the world and realise they have the power to change it.'

KNOWHOW

If you have a job, make sure you are being paid the right amount for it. If you are not, consider asking your employer for a pay rise or find a similar job that pays better. Recruitment websites such as Indeed (www.indeed.co.uk/salaries) and Michael Page (www.michaelpage.co.uk) have free online salary comparison tools.

Your personal circumstances

Sometimes the hand that life has dealt you isn't quite as perfect as you would have liked it to be. You may find yourself having to deal with all kinds of issues and problems – illness, disability, divorce, debt, the need to care for others, lack of family support, housing problems, geographical issues, language and cultural barriers – that threaten to overshadow your desire to be successful. It can be hard to focus on your goals when there are other big things taking up space in your life and demanding your time and energy.

Fortunately, it is not impossible to triumph over the odds

to achieve something amazing – and there are many examples of successful people who have done so.

While it may be hard to completely ignore the obstacle in your way, you may be able to find a way of creating a path round it. Dyslexia, for example, is a type of learning disability that can make it difficult to read or write because letters can appear jumbled. However, to offset this, many dyslexic people have above-average strengths in skills such as big-picture thinking, lateral thinking and problem solving, as well as visual strengths and an intuitive understanding of how things work. All this means that they are frequently successful in entrepreneurship, sales, art and design, acting, engineering, architecture, IT, computer animation and practical trades.

Richard Branson has dyslexia and dropped out of school at the age of 16 because his teachers saw it as a handicap and thought he was lazy and dumb. However, he has gone on to be a highly successful entrepreneur, creating the Virgin group, which consists of 400 companies. He has amassed a personal fortune of £4.9 billion. In a piece for *The Sunday Times* he wrote: 'It is time we lost the stigma around dyslexia. It is not a disadvantage; it is merely a different way of thinking. Once freed from archaic schooling practices and preconceptions, my mind opened up. Out in the real world, my dyslexia became my massive advantage: it helped me to think creatively and laterally, and see solutions where others saw problems.'

If you are trying to reach your goal while also battling difficult personal circumstances, take it slowly and be kind to yourself. Your battle should not be with yourself. While it might take you a bit longer to get where you want to be, it doesn't actually matter. This isn't a race.

KNOWHOW

Seek out relevant organisations that may be able to assist you with programmes, mentoring, advice, or even grants and loans. The Prince's Trust (www. princes-trust.org.uk), for example, provides support to disadvantaged young people aged 13 to 30 to help them get into jobs, education or training. Disability Rights UK (www.disabilityrightsuk.org) has a lot of information and advice about education, skills and employment for people with disabilities on its website. The British Dyslexia Association (www.bdadyslexia.org.uk) offers advice on how to cope in the workplace, and also on apprenticeships. EmployAbility (www.employ-ability.org.uk) offers opportunities for disabled and dyslexic students and graduates, and DisabilityJobSite (www. disabilityjobsite.co.uk) has a database of job vacancies for people with disabilities.

NOW TAKE ACTION

1. Write a list of the obstacles that you think could be standing in your way.

2. Now study your list. Are there any obstacles that you might be able to find a way round, perhaps by taking a different route or ignoring them altogether? Are there any that you yourself have inadvertently placed in your path and that, in fact, have no right to be there?

3. Be honest with yourself. If your obstacle wasn't there would you feel pleased and relieved, or would you feel scared now that there was nothing to stop you getting on with achieving your dream?

—————————

Chapter 6

Begin developing good habits

*'Don't judge each day by the harvest you reap,
but by the seeds you plant'*

Robert Louis Stevenson, writer

Every single day you are gradually shaping the person you will be in the future. It's a crazy thought, but of course it's true. The idea is both daunting and exciting. So, as well as negotiating any possible obstacles in your way, a highly effective way to improve your chances of success is to start developing good habits. That's because playing to your strengths is not just about making the big dramatic moves; it is also about making small but important changes every day that can steadily take you to where you want to be. All those changes will add up, even if you can't initially see the differences you are making.

Developing good habits is a bit like drawing two straight lines which have a very small angle between them. At the point where the two lines meet, you can barely see the difference between them. But as the lines start to move further away from their meeting point, the gap between them becomes more noticeable, until it becomes clear the two lines are heading off in completely different directions. You may not immediately notice the difference your good habits are making, but you will.

Let's take a look at how to introduce new habits into your life that will really make a difference to your ability to get to where you want to be.

Make 'change' your new routine

It is easy to get stuck in a rut when you are doing the same thing every day. As the days merge into an indistinguishable blur, it can become impossible to imagine doing something different. Make a conscious effort to shake things up every now and then to kickstart new thoughts and ideas. Take a different route to work, try a new form of exercise, buy your clothes from a different shop.

Even the simplest changes can have a big impact. Drax is an executive search firm in London that specialises in finding senior management teams for private equity-backed businesses. It gets its 35 employees to swap desks every few months to keep them thinking in a fresh and vibrant way. Every single person in the company takes part in the move, including the senior partners. It takes place at 3pm on a Friday and each time no one has any idea where they will end up sitting, or whom they will end up sitting next to.

Managing partner Graham Roadnight says the regular move strengthens relationships within the firm and generates a much stronger sense of teamwork, because people begin talking to the new colleagues sitting near them, sharing ideas and making new connections.

He says, 'We think there are a lot of benefits to doing this. It gives everyone a real appreciation of how other people work and people communicate with each other better. In an office people tend to put up lots of individual barriers, but this helps to break them down. We feel that mixing everyone up in this way is a really positive thing for the company. It benefits everyone involved.'

Start putting extra effort into everything you do

Extra effort rarely goes unrewarded. Most of the time the right people will notice, provided you take the time to show them what they should be looking at.

Andy Evans really wanted to get a job as a videographer with Social Chain, an innovative social-media marketing agency in Manchester. But there were no job vacancies advertised on their website, and anyway he had heard that Social Chain's chief executive Steve Bartlett liked people who were looking for a job to find a way of showing their creativity rather than simply sending in a CV.

So, when Andy found out that Social Chain had won an award for being the best social-media agency for two years in a row, he decided to mark the occasion by sending them an enormous orange helium-filled balloon in the shape of a flying fish. He attached a memory stick to the balloon. The memory stick contained a video message of him saying 'Congratulations, you are now a big fish!' In the video he also asked for a job and included examples of his work, with a link to his Snapchat account.

He persuaded someone from Social Chain to let him into

the building and flew his fish balloon around their offices, guiding it via remote control from a hidden position outside the door.

He says, 'They couldn't see me, they could only see this big fish flying through the front door. I wanted to create a bit of intrigue.'

His efforts paid off. A week later Steve Bartlett got in touch and invited Andy for an interview. He asked Andy to do a day's trial filming and then offered him a job. Andy, who is known as Doddz, now travels with Steve around the world videoing him for a daily vlog, which he edits and uploads every evening onto YouTube and shares on social media.

He says, 'It is hard work, but it is amazing. I am so glad I went to all that effort.'

Make time for creative play

Remember playing at the sand and water table at nursery school? Or mashing up plasticine into an interesting sludge colour? Well, it turns out that getting messy and creative wasn't just great fun, it was also busy sparking your synapses and giving your brain the chance to come up with lots of new and interesting thoughts.

The good news is that creative play works for adults too.

In its early days Google introduced a '20 per cent Time' policy that allowed all its employees to spend 20 per cent of their working hours, equivalent to one day a week, on independent projects of their own.

Explaining the policy, Google founders Larry Page and Sergey Brin wrote, 'We encourage our employees, in addition to their regular projects, to spend 20 per cent of their time working on what they think will most benefit Google. This empowers them to be more creative and innovative. Many of our significant advances have happened in this manner.'

It worked too – it is thought that 20 per cent Time led to the development of Google projects such as Google News, Gmail and AdSense.

Inspired by Google's example, other tech companies launched creativity programmes of their own. Apple introduced Blue Sky, which allowed workers to spend a few weeks on pet projects, and Microsoft created The Garage, a space for employees to build their own products using Microsoft resources.

As Google has morphed from a maverick start-up to a large corporation, inevitably the reality of its 20 per cent Time policy has dwindled as it has become harder for employees to find the time away from their main jobs to pursue side projects. But the concept has left a strong imprint. As Laszlo Bock, the former head of Google's People Operations, explains: 'In some ways, the idea of 20 per cent Time is more important than the reality of it.'

You too can create your own 20 per cent Time. If you're in a full-time job, consider keeping one day a week completely clear of meetings, to give your mind some space to think about your job and how you can make it more interesting and fulfilling. Being able to work at your own pace on something, without having to watch the clock in order to be somewhere else at a certain time, will be enormously refreshing. Try to keep the same day each week meeting-free, so you can start to anticipate and build that thinking time into your regular routine.

Or how about setting aside one evening a week after work to do something fun and different to get your creative thoughts flowing – learn how to paint, or make pots, or even take a trampolining class. Evening classes are a great way to do this as you can do something different each term without it costing you a fortune – check out your local adult education institute or visit Floodlight (www.floodlight.co.uk), which lists adult evening classes around the country.

There's another reason why being creative is such a good thing – there's a proven link between creativity and positivity. In 2016, researchers at the University of Otago in New Zealand found that engaging in a creative activity just once a day can lead to a more positive state of mind. The researchers looked at the responses of 658 young adults to find out if creativity has an effect on emotional well-being. They discovered that there was an 'upward spiral for well-being and creativity' in those individuals who engaged in daily creative pastimes.

Start gathering allies

Look around your place of work or your life and identify the people who are supporting you and encouraging you. Now look again, because there is also likely to be another team of people that could be supporting and encouraging you if only you made the effort to get to know them, to understand them and to discover how their aspirations might fit in with yours.

Don't confine yourself to seeking out people your age, or at your level, or in the same department or function – take advantage of any company-wide team-building events or combined projects to make bonds and links to people in other areas of the business. The more people you can gather to help you on your way, whether practically, or through advice or recommendation, or mentoring, the better.

Make sure too that you come across as the kind of person whom someone might actually want to help and support. I was recently sent an email from someone asking for my help with a survey they were doing. It ended with the words: *'So will you do me a favour of taking two minutes to tell me what's important to you? It'll mean a lot to me if you tell me your thoughts here. It's good to be in touch again. I'm really looking forward to hearing from you.'*

How lovely, I thought, and I was all set to click on the link and offer my opinion until I read further down the email to the PS. It said, *'PS I'm always impressed when someone does something instantly. The high achievers I know complete tasks quickly in order to move on. So even though you're busy, I really appreciate you taking two minutes to tell me your thoughts.'*

At which point I thought something unprintable and deleted the email. This person was asking me to spare my time and effort to help them for nothing in return, so it felt incredibly rude of them to then come over all passive aggressive and demand that I help them instantly – with the veiled threat that if I didn't then I couldn't be classed as a high achiever. It was short-sighted too. I wonder how many other people who received the email almost took part in the survey, but didn't when they read that.

Concepts such as politeness, courtesy, good manners and punctuality may seem quaint and old-fashioned these days, but they still matter, and they can do much to improve your chances of achieving more in life. Send a thank-you note, reply to invitations, remember people's names, smile. Play nice. It doesn't take much, but people will remember you.

Jonathan Shalit is a highly regarded talent manager and the chairman of ROAR Global Entertainment Group. Over the years he has worked with many hugely successful international stars including Katherine Jenkins, Elton John, Cher, Emma Bunton and Charlotte Church, and was awarded an OBE for services to the entertainment industry.

Jonathan says good manners and old-fashioned courtesy make a big difference, whether that is arriving in good time for an audition or responding promptly to an invitation.

He says, 'The person who leaves last and arrives first is going to have more chance than the person who arrives last and leaves first. And so is the person who is always polite. Doing anything that takes you beyond the competition always holds you in good stead and gives you more opportunities. If people like you, then even if they say no to you the first time round, they might regret saying no and there might be an opportunity in the future to say yes.'

He adds, 'Make sure that the people who make decisions are well disposed towards you. Always leave a room with the people in that room liking you and wanting to see you again. Always end a telephone conversation with someone wanting to take your call in the future. Always make sure that in an email correspondence someone wants to read your email next time.'

Jonathan says everyone can benefit from being charming and nice, no matter what stage they are at in life: 'If you are in the fortunate position of being the only person in the world who can do something, then I guess you can get away with being less likeable and less co-operative. But I can't think of any opportunity in the world where there is not a choice between you and someone else. And if there is a choice, a producer or director is more likely to choose someone who is going to be reliable, who is going to turn up on time, and who will be fully committed to the opportunity, than someone who has a reputation for being unreliable, late, rude or uncooperative.'

Channel Nora Ephron

Nora Ephron was a brilliant US screenwriter, who wrote the hit films *When Harry Met Sally, Sleepless in Seattle* and *Silkwood*. She believed that every aspect of life was potentially useful, and her family's catchphrase, which she took as her own, was 'Everything is copy.' In other words, everything that happens to you, or to other people you know, is potentially useful in some way, even if you don't immediately know why.

You don't have to be a screenwriter or novelist to realise that this is a brilliant motto to use in life. It's reassuring too, to think that all those mishaps, failures and disasters are not entirely pointless.

Start tuning in to what other people around you are talking about, and take note of anything interesting – events that are taking place, magazine articles, useful websites. And go to reunions for your school, university and work, even if you hate the idea. I went to a reunion at my old school recently for the first time since I'd left, and it was truly awful. But then I went to a university reunion a few weeks later and it was fantastic. In fact, one of the people I chatted to there has ended up in this book.

Start being less predictable

Start trying out things you would never normally do. Wear different styles of clothing, go on a different type of holiday, read a different kind of book.

There are two reasons for doing this. First, so that you get used to being unpredictable, and second, so that the people around you get used to it too.

The less people can pigeonhole you and stereotype you, the less they will expect you to behave in a certain way, and the freer you will be to pursue your own path in life. If other people are able to say, 'But you always . . .', 'But you never . . .', then you are constantly going to find it very difficult to do anything new because it will clash with their image of you and you will have to deal with their shock and incredulity on top of everything else.

Doing one thing that is bold and different enables you to do more things that are bold and different. The first time you do something unusual, all your friends will talk about it. The second time you do it, they will talk about it less. The third time they will barely even bother mentioning it, and will just see you instead as the person who likes trying new things. 'Oh, don't worry about her, she's always doing mad stuff,' they will say. And then you will be free to create your own life.

Build in some quiet times

Everyone seems to take a great deal of pride in being busy these days, and particularly in telling everyone else how busy they are as they cancel meetings and appointments at the last minute because they just don't have the time. It can get to the point where anyone who is not busy being busy can start to feel that they are missing out. Indeed, a fascinating survey by marketing firm Havas Worldwide in 2015 of 10,000 people in 28 countries found that the idea of being busy is so valued that 40 per cent of respondents admitted to sometimes pretending to be busier than they are, while 60 per cent believed that other people were faking being busy too. As the authors of the report note, 'Our issue with time seems to be not so much that we have too little of it, but that we now equate being busy with leading a life of significance. And we don't want to be relegated to the sidelines. Whereas leisure was once regarded as an important time for reflection, introspection, and the pursuit of the "finer things" in life, free time is now seen as an admission that you're nonessential.'

But being busy does not equal achievement. Indeed, being busy can actually stand in the way of you achieving your goals because it stops you having the freedom or time to think up the good ideas.

So make sure you are not filling up your time with pointless busy-ness just for the sake of it, and deliberately start building slabs of nothing into your week. Once you have stopped running around like the Duracell bunny in the adverts, you might surprise yourself with what you can achieve.

In a recent magazine interview Michael Lewis, the best-selling author of *Liar's Poker* and *Moneyball*, said he can easily spend hours doing very little at all – and years finding out huge amounts about people that he never eventually writes about. But that's all fine. He says, 'People waste years of their lives not being willing to waste hours of their lives. If you mistake busy-ness for importance – which we do a lot – you're not able to see what really is important.'

Start looking for the upside

Things are not always going to go your way. They are just not. That job you wanted goes to someone else, that plane you needed to catch is cancelled, that prototype you created doesn't work, the important phone call you have been waiting for all week comes through while you are on a train, just as you are about to go into a tunnel. It's called life and it can sometimes be infuriating.

But it is good to try to keep a sense of humour when everything around you falls apart, and not just because it's better for your blood pressure. The fact is that you don't know what's around the corner, and it may be that the very thing going wrong is about to cause something even better to go right.

There are all kinds of amazing things that were accidentally invented when something went wrong. Post-It notes were made from glue that didn't stick properly, Playdoh was made from wallpaper cleaner that didn't work, cornflakes were created when John Kellogg and his brother forgot about some wheat they had cooked and tried to turn it into sheets of dough. Microwave ovens, slinky toys that walk downstairs and even penicillin were created from a mistake.

So give yourself a break. Wait a while before you judge any outcome or situation and then focus on the good stuff that happened, not on the stuff that didn't quite work out.

Ditch the stuff you hate

Sometimes the ebb and flow of your life just carries you along and you end up doing things that you really don't like, over and over again, simply because you've always done them and because it seems like too much effort to make a change. But that's such a waste of energy.

So take a few minutes to stop and think about which bits you love about your life, and which you don't. Now ask yourself, would it really matter if you gave them a miss? Take Halloween. Do you actually like Halloween? I hate Halloween. There's nothing nice about Halloween, with its gruesome costumes and dubious practice of encouraging children to knock on strangers' doors and accept sweets from them. Personally

I don't think it has any feature whatsoever to redeem it. Far nicer to draw the curtains, put on a funny film, cut out the scary middle man and give the kids a bag of sweets yourself instead. So follow my lead and bin whatever it is that you hate. Stop getting involved. You will feel so much happier.

Allow room for the magic to happen

The most exciting thing about life is the part that is unknowable and untameable, the bit that allows for the chance meeting, the random phone call, the surprise runaway success. Right now there are hundreds of communications agencies out there desperately trying to work out how to make a YouTube clip go viral, or get a book onto the bestseller lists, or make a product suddenly become the ultimate must-have item and fly off the shelves.

But the truth is there is no magic formula. No matter how much someone might pretend to be able to control social media reaction or influence word-of-mouth opinion, no matter how much a publisher might dream of finding the next big thing, ultimately it is all down to chance, magic and random star dust. Which means that the next big thing could just as easily be you.

One of my favourite things in the world of business is the idea of unicorns. Not the magical mythical creatures that look like horses with a long spike on their forehead, but the name given to privately held start-up companies that are valued at over US $1 billion. I particularly like the idea of serious business people in dark suits sitting around an executive boardroom talking about unicorns with a straight face.

It's an incredibly hard thing to achieve a value of more than $1 billion as a start-up business. Most start-ups don't even survive past their third birthday and those that do can take years to achieve any kind of size or value, which makes these business unicorns pretty special and incredibly rare. Indeed, the name was originally coined in 2013 by venture capitalist Aileen Lee to reflect their almost mythical status. But the point is, unlike the fairytale unicorns, they are not mythical at all. They do actually exist. In fact there have been a total of 229 of them created in the world so far, including Skyscanner, Snapchat and Dropbox.

Rarity makes them special. But it doesn't make them impossible, nor any less real. Life-changing success can come to anyone, from any direction, at any time. Allow room for the magic to happen. Because then it just might.

NOW TAKE ACTION

1. Look at your daily routine. Is it possible to shake it up and introduce some variety into it?

2. Stop being busy for the sake of it. Look at what you do each day. Are there things you do simply to fill in time?

3. Think about how you might introduce some creativity into your life. Knit yourself a scarf, or make someone a birthday card instead of buying one from a shop.

Chapter 7

Start thinking in a different way

'Impossible is not a fact. It's an opinion. Impossible is not a declaration. It's a dare. Impossible is potential. Impossible is temporary. Impossible is nothing'

Muhammad Ali, boxer

Good news – you now have everything in place to enable you to start making changes to your life and work. You've established your vision and the direction you want to go in, you've identified your strengths, and you've understood how you can overcome obstacles and establish the good habits that are going to get you moving forwards. What you need now is to understand just how much power and heft you can add to the process, simply by changing the way you think. Now is the time to put any doubts you may have to one side because thinking positively is not just a pleasant way to live, it can actually change an outcome for the better.

There is an extraordinary show on ITV called *This Time Next Year*, which is presented by Davina McCall. Her guests arrive on stage through the first door with a massive challenge ahead of them, which they are determined to achieve over the next year. Losing ten stone, perhaps, or learning to speak without a stammer, or competing in the Paralympics.

When the guest has left the stage through the door they came in, Davina walks over to the second door. Then, using the magic of television, the same person who has seemingly just left the stage through the first door immediately reappears through the second door. But this time it is a year later and here they are having achieved their goal. The woman who wanted to lose ten stone has miraculously shed it, the man who wanted to be able to speak more easily can now do so.

It is mind-blowing television. The studio looks exactly the same, Davina looks exactly the same, wearing the same dress and with the same hair style, and seamlessly walks from one door to the other. Yet her guest is utterly transformed.

And it is the most remarkable visual reminder that everyone has the power within them to make big achievements happen.

Never forget, you are capable of fantastic, amazing and lasting change. Indeed, perhaps the single biggest adjustment you can make within yourself is to realise that you really can do this. All you need to do is start realising that you are in the driving seat of your life, and that you can take control of the steering wheel and take off in any direction you want to go.

Let's take a look at how you can do this.

See the bigger picture

It's easy to get so bogged down in the small challenges of life that you forget to think bigger. But you should. Not long ago I was travelling on the London Underground and

I couldn't help overhearing the conversation between two people standing near me. The man was clearly upset and the woman was trying to calm him down. As I listened I realised that both of them worked for the same company, and that the man was unhappy because another colleague had just been promoted to a Level Five position, while he was still stuck on Level Four. He felt that this was particularly unfair, because the person who had been promoted hadn't been working at the company for as long as he had. Meanwhile, the woman was trying to cheer him up by saying that if he worked hard, he could be promoted to Level Five himself in 18 months or so. But that prospect simply sent him into even greater gloom and fury.

As they continued to talk, it struck me how restricted their horizons were. Instead of obsessing about how to get to Level Five, whatever that was, the man should have been working out how to bypass Level Five altogether and jump straight to Level Six. Or Eight. Even better, he should have been focusing on finding another job where he was actually excited about the work he was doing rather than what level he was on. The problem was that he had become so enmeshed in the structure of the company he worked for, and so focused on the idea that this structure was in some way important, he couldn't see beyond it to the bigger picture, or the bigger goal.

Think about where your life is heading right now. Are the goals you are aiming for really your goals, or are they simply something your employer or someone else has put in place for you to aspire to? What is the best you can achieve on the path you are on – and is it enough for you?

Stamp on any negativity

Negativity is catching, and reinforcing, and generally bad. If you find yourself going over the same old arguments in your head about why you are likely to fail at something, or why an idea will never work, check yourself and consciously stop allowing those thoughts to fill your head. Instead, introduce a more neutral idea to fill the gap that the negative thoughts have left behind, something that keeps the door open to the possibility that good things could happen. How about: 'I'll give it a try', 'It might work', 'I'll take the first step and see what happens.'

The more you can move the dial towards a position of optimism and hope, the more you pave the way for you to achieve fantastic things.

Get rid of the distractions

Before you can achieve anything worthwhile, you need to deal with the little niggly tasks – those small annoying things that nag away at the back of your mind which you never quite get round to. Stop letting them get in the way. Just set aside a couple of hours to deal with them and sort them out. They could be things that are as mundane as buying a new kettle, completing your tax return and getting a dental filling repaired. Whatever they are, get them done, because right now they are taking up valuable space in your head that you need to devote to more important tasks. Getting the niggles off the agenda will not only clear your mind of unnecessary clutter, you'll also feel calmer and more in control, and more able to deal with whatever interesting things life throws your way.

Get organised

When you start playing to your strengths, your life and career might start taking off in ways you never imagined. So you need to make sure your personal admin systems are already set up. That might mean making sure you have enough printer ink in the house, or that your passport is valid, or that you know where your driving licence is. Or ensuring that you have an up-to-date CV stored on your computer ready to send out at a moment's notice. You can download a free CV template from the Total Jobs website (www.totaljobs.com) – the site has seven templates that cover most situations, from being unemployed, to looking for your first job, to getting back into the workplace after a career break.

Start looking outwards

There is a big wide world of potential out there. Start opening your mind to new possibilities by finding out what other people are up to. A simple way to do this is to attend free events – for example, many libraries and universities organise talks by people from all walks of life, who have interesting or inspiring stories to tell or wisdom to impart. Manchester University, for example, runs many free events that are open to anyone, including debates at its Alliance Manchester Business School and entrepreneur talks at its Manchester Business Centre. You can find details on the Manchester University website (www.manchester.ac.uk). Check out the websites of organisations located near you to find out what is on offer in your area.

Work out what your priorities are

If you are serious about achieving more, then in some other area of your life or work you are going to need to achieve less. That may mean spending fewer hours on social media, or watching less television, or socialising less often with friends. Think hard about what your key priorities are, in order to avoid getting side-tracked by all the other things you could be spending your time on. Decide what matters most to you. If you want to save money to go travelling, but also love going out with friends every night, for example, then something is going to have to give.

The Spanish painter Diego Velázquez was a brilliant artist, but he got so caught up in climbing the hierarchy of the royal court of King Philip in Madrid that he ended up having less and less time to paint. As Laura Cumming writes in her book *The Vanishing Man*, 'Velázquez accepted court positions that took him away from art all through his life. His industry as a royal servant is distressing to this day, since it speaks of all the pictures he never had time to paint.'

He eventually rose to the position of King's High Chamberlain, Holder of the Palace Key, the pinnacle of a courtier's career, and was appointed to the high order of the Knights of Santiago, so perhaps rising through the court really was more important to him than painting. We will never know. But if you have big things to achieve, make sure you don't fritter away your time and energy on activities that are less important to you.

Be ready to seize the moment

Make sure you are prepared and ready to take leaps and bounds towards your goals whenever they present themselves, because exciting opportunities are unlikely to hang around for long.

Natasha Barnes was playing the part of Fanny Brice's dresser in the West End musical *Funny Girl* and was also the understudy to Sheridan Smith, who was playing the leading role of Fanny Brice. Then one evening at 7.10pm Natasha was told she would be playing the leading role for real – at 8pm.

It was a scary moment. She was about to perform in front of an audience that had paid a lot of money for its tickets in the expectation that it would be seeing Sheridan Smith, and Natasha had never even performed the show all the way through. But she didn't just survive the experience, she was brilliant at it and even got a standing ovation. She also got rave reviews from the critics. The *Daily Telegraph*'s theatre critic Dominic Cavendish gave her five stars, writing, 'The upside of Smith's no-show is the discovery of Barnes. The 25-year-old isn't just a serviceable stand-in, she's a sensation in her own right.'

People started buying tickets specifically to see Natasha perform the leading role, and now she has become a star herself in a nationwide tour of the show – as the lead. Or as she tweeted, 'I don't recognise my life at all anymore ... It's like a really, really good episode of a great TV series.'

You too never know when it will be your big moment. You may not be asked to take over the main part in a West End show, but you may need to cover for your boss at short notice, or stand in for someone running an event, or take over a project halfway through. So make sure you are ready to do it brilliantly, in the best way you possibly can.

Start making every day count

When I was 22 I worked in the marketing division of a large oil company in Sydney, Australia, for a few months in order to earn enough money to pay for my return trip home. It was an eye-opening introduction into the corporate world. I never really worked out what everyone did, but I vividly remember one man in our department who hated his job with a passion.

I know this because he told everyone at every opportunity just how much he loathed it. In my youthful naivety I couldn't understand why he didn't just leave and get a job elsewhere. Then, one day I overheard him talking to a colleague, saying cheerfully that at least he only had ten more years to go until he could get his full company pension and leave. Ten more years of doing a job he absolutely hated just for that? What a crazy waste of a life. Even then it struck me as being sad and pointless. And now, having realised how fast life zooms past, it strikes me as being even more so.

Taking hold of your life and sending it off in the direction you want it to go is a very exciting thing to do. At times it will be fun, challenging, illuminating, thrilling, unpredictable, demanding, fascinating and amazing. It is also an incredible privilege, because for previous generations, and indeed for many people in other parts of the world right now where lives are more restricted and controlled, it simply would not be possible. My grandmother really wanted to be a librarian, a fairly modest ambition, but her father forbade her from pursuing her dream because he did not approve of the idea. And so that was the end of it. It seems extraordinary now.

We are so lucky to have not only the choice but the freedom to decide how our life turns out and it is important not to take that for granted. Every step you take towards a better, more fulfilled life is not just a personal step for you, it is a big thumbs up for humanity, and a celebration of being alive, and of having the most amazing opportunities to do brilliant things. We should never forget that.

NOW TAKE ACTION

1. Work out how many hours a day you spend on social media or watching television. You may be shocked.

2. Identify the other distractions in your life and see if there is a way of reducing or eliminating them in favour of doing something more worthwhile – including getting organised.

3. Talk to your parents and, if possible, your grandparents about what they wanted to achieve in life, and how far they have succeeded in doing so. Find out what helped them, and what held them back, and in what way life has changed since they were young. It will be eye-opening.

Chapter 8

Start taking control

'Choice, not chance, determines your destiny'

Aristotle, philosopher

Sometimes getting ahead in life can feel as though it is an endless succession of putting important decisions in other people's hands. Applying for a job, sitting an exam, submitting a proposal, competing for a place on a course – to take just some examples – can all feel as though someone else has the final say on whether you succeed or fail. Worst of all, these are often people you have never met and don't know anything about; and who don't know anything about you. This can feel disheartening, disempowering, and if things don't go as you would like them to, very annoying.

The truth is that you can't control other people's decisions. But, you can control your own decisions. And those decisions can give you more power than you think in determining how a situation unfolds around you.

One of my favourite films is *Strictly Ballroom*, which tells the story of Australian ballroom dancer Scott Hastings. He decides that he is fed up with following traditional ballroom dance moves and wants to make up his own steps instead.

His mother is horrified and so is the president of the Australian Dance Federation, who declares firmly that 'There are no new steps.' Everyone is against him – Scott's regular dance partner refuses to enter any more competitions with him and the only person who is prepared to dance with him is frumpy Fran from the beginners' class. But Scott loves the idea of creating something new on his own terms, so the two of them practise in secret, incorporating the lively Spanish Paso Doble dance into the routine they create.

Despite much opposition, they eventually succeed in dancing their own steps at the Pan-Pacific Grand Prix Ballroom Championships. They have done it their way, and while it might not have pleased everyone, their sense of achievement is joyful to see.

It's time to look at how you can take control of how your life turns out – and in particular at situations in which you unthinkingly give that control away, and how you might get it back.

Do it yourself

If you are finding it impossible to break into the industry you would like to be in, and are facing continual rejections from people already in it, consider whether there is a way to cut out other people altogether and to do what you want to do without anyone else's approval, agreement or acceptance. They may be barring the front door, but see whether there might be a side window you could climb through instead.

Mel Sherratt had wanted to be a writer ever since she was a child and won a creative writing competition at the age of eleven. As an adult she began writing short stories for magazines in the hope that they would publish them, but had little success. She then wrote her first novel and sent out the manuscript to literary agents in the hope of getting it published. But as the years passed, the rejection letters began to mount up. So, she reluctantly gave up her dream of writing for a living and became a local authority housing officer, before getting a job in training and development. Mel continued to write in her spare time, though, and when she was made redundant she took a year out of paid employment to concentrate on writing full time.

She wrote a crime thriller called *Taunting the Dead*, but once again publishers rejected it. So at the end of 2011 she decided to take matters into her own hands and self-publish it as an e-book on Kindle.

Mel says, 'I'd tried for 12 years, with two different agents, to get my books published with traditional publishers. I saw a few self-published writers having a go and doing well, so I decided to self-publish *Taunting the Dead*, and then maybe off the back of any sales I had, a publisher might be interested. I didn't want to wait any longer, and continual rejection is hard to get over. Doing something positive, rather than sitting back and waiting, was a make-or-break move.'

She shared the news in a blog she wrote on her website and within six weeks her book had entered the Kindle UK top ten. It stayed there for 16 weeks. Mel quickly self-published three more novels that she had written as a series, *The Estate Series*, and they too headed straight into the Kindle top ten. By the end of 2012, just a year after she had started self-publishing, she had sold over 200,000 books online.

Mel has now published 12 novels, all of which have become bestsellers, and she has sold almost a million books. And somewhat ironically, her success at self-publishing has at last attracted the attention of a traditional book publisher, and her books are now published as paperbacks too.

Mel says, 'I always call *Taunting the Dead* my door opener. Without self-publishing that, I might never have started on this fantastic journey. It took a lot of courage to press the publish button, but I'm so glad I did. I still wake up feeling lucky.'

KNOWHOW

If you've written a brilliant book but are finding it hard to find a publisher, then you could publish it yourself, either as an e-book, or as an actual paperback, or both. The simplest way to do this is through Amazon's self-publishing programme KDP, which will also automatically list your book for sale on the Amazon website (www.amazon.co.uk or www.amazon.com). The process is completely free, even to publish your book as a paperback, because the book is printed on demand whenever a customer orders a copy. You also receive royalties for every book sold. Go to Amazon's website, scroll down to the bottom and click on 'Independently publish with us' to find out more.

Go direct

For many of the things we do in life, we voluntarily, and often unthinkingly, hand over control to some kind of intermediary stationed somewhere between us and our goal. It may be an organisation, it may be a website or an app, or it may be something else. The tendency to do this is increasing as people do more and more online. In theory, these intermediaries are there to help us, by providing information, by simplifying processes and by saving us time, and that gives us the illusion that we are still in charge. But you only have to feel the enormous sense of helplessness and frustration when a connection is lost, a payment doesn't go through or a transaction fails to upload to know that it can also make you feel even more helpless and out of control than before.

Fortunately, it is possible to take back control – by communicating with real people, by going direct to the source, by turning yourself into the one with the power to say yes.

If you are looking for a job, for example, don't just upload your CV onto a raft of job-finding websites and hope for the best. These websites claim to simplify the job-finding process by enabling you to search through their databases using your chosen criteria, by allowing you to apply for positions directly through their websites and by promising to alert potential employers to your existence. But the reality is that you may well find yourself left in the dark, not getting any response to your applications and having no idea about how close or not you were to getting a job.

So wherever possible, give the intermediaries a miss and deal directly with your target. Draw up a list of companies you'd like to work for and check out their websites. Most companies now list their specific vacancies so you can just apply for the jobs you are interested in directly. Virgin Media (www. virginmedia.com), for example, currently lists over 200 job vacancies on its website, which are searchable by keyword and location. You can often also follow big employers on Twitter to get instant alerts when new vacancies arise – some of them even have job-specific Twitter accounts.

If it's a smaller company that interests you, find out the name of the managing director and send him or her a short email. You'd be surprised how impressed people are when someone shows a bit of initiative.

Start living your life for you, not for your CV

When you are trying to get ahead in your career, it can be tempting to make job decisions based on what might look good on your CV or resumé, rather than what you actually want to do with your life. Especially when everyone around you is doing the same thing.

But there comes a point when you have to start living life in a way that makes sense to you instinctively, rather than in a way that second guesses what a potential employer might want to hear.

Andy Vaughan understood this. By the age of 39, Andy was a highly respected chief executive, having enjoyed a fast-track career at ICL, the computer firm, before leading a management buyout of one of its subsidiaries. He successfully grew the business to such an extent that when it was sold it made its backers 14 times their initial investment.

It was an impressive achievement, particularly at such a relatively young age, and most people in his situation would have immediately thrown themselves into another big role, spending every waking hour at work, often at the expense of their personal lives.

But Andy realised he didn't want to just live to work. And most importantly he realised that he was in the fortunate financial position of being able consciously to choose how he wanted to live. So instead of simply picking another high-powered executive role from the lucrative offers coming his way, much to everyone's surprise he decided to step away from the high-pressure work environment for a while and take his wife and young family to live in a remote part of Portugal instead.

He says, 'I wanted to extract myself completely and have a real break. I had got so engrossed on the treadmill of growing a business, I had forgotten what was important to me and what really mattered. I had money in the bank, two fantastic little boys and a wife I loved, and I realised that what my family really needed now most was to have me around.'

Andy and his wife bought a house within days of arriving in Portugal and for the first two years he did no work at all, spending all his time with his family. Then, he began to look for work back in the UK, but his priorities had shifted. He deliberately chose to take on part-time non-executive chairman roles of private-equity backed businesses, which would enable him to work with flexibility, and so maintain a healthy balance between his work and his family.

He says, 'I didn't want work to define me. I wanted to be a really good dad and a really good husband and then somewhere down the line, not a bad businessman. Whereas up to that point I had that completely on its head. It was a real change for me.'

After five years away the family returned to live full time in the UK, but their time in Portugal left a lasting impression on Andy. He says, 'I look back on it and it was the best thing I ever did. It had an effect on every aspect of my life and I think about it every day.'

Neither has it held him back in any way career-wise. Andy now has an extremely successful career as a chairman in the private equity sector and since returning from Portugal has overseen the sale of eight private equity-backed businesses, making him one of only a handful of people in the UK to achieve this.

Listen to your gut

Your gut instinct is the thought you have almost before you've had time to decide what you think, and as such it can really help you tap into your true feelings about something – whether that be a person, a place or a situation. It is a mixture of logic and emotion and it can be a surprisingly powerful way to take control of where you are heading, if you listen to it carefully.

Holly Tucker is the co-founder of NotontheHighStreet.com, a highly successful online marketplace that sells crafts and homewares made by small businesses. She now runs Holly and Co (www.holly.co), a business she set up in 2017 to provide advice and inspiration for small businesses. She regularly makes decisions based on her gut instinct.

She says, 'Your gut instinct is like having your own crystal ball. It is your inner energy, thoughts and intelligence, all coming together to try and break through the noise to tell you something. And the more you listen to it, the more you are training it and the easier it becomes to hear what it is saying. Every time I listen to my gut instinct, it turns out to be the right decision, and every time I have ignored it, the decision has been the wrong one, 100 per cent of the time.'

Holly finds listening to her gut instinct particularly useful when deciding who to work with. She says, 'I gave one of our personal assistants at NotontheHighStreet the opportunity to head up a new area of the business because I instinctively felt she had untapped potential. Everyone in the HR department was very nervous about my decision because gut instinct is not something that you can justify by showing it on an Excel spreadsheet. But she turned out to be amazing. Every time I ignored my gut feeling and hired someone who had an impressive CV, but whom I did not instinctively feel was right for the business, 100 per cent of the time these people didn't work out. Not listening to my gut was not only painful, it was also expensive.'

Make your own decisions

Don't unthinkingly hand over control to other people by letting them make important decisions on your behalf, simply because you don't have time to think the issues through yourself, or because you don't think it matters much. Sometimes other people have different motivations and agendas to you, either consciously or subconsciously, and the decisions they make might not be right for your situation and circumstances.

The National Environment Research Council learnt this the hard way. When they decided to ask the British public what they should call their brand-new £200 million Royal polar research ship, they presumably imagined the suggestions would be suitably inspiring and prestigious, in line with the names given to their four other Royal research ships – *Ernest Shackleton*, *James Cook*, *James Clark Ross* and *Discovery*. However, the council, a British government agency, had underestimated the British public's enthusiasm for absurdity and mischief-making. Instead of choosing another celebrated explorer, the public overwhelmingly voted to call the ship *Boaty McBoatface*, with so many people voting for it online that the website crashed.

Faced with the prospect of the ship at the forefront of

British naval engineering becoming a laughing stock, an embarrassed government minister eventually decided to ignore the results of the public vote and call the ship *Sir David Attenborough*, after the popular naturalist. Instead, they gave the name *Boaty McBoatface* to a bright yellow remote-controlled submarine that lives on the ship.

It's a funny story, but there's an important message here too. When people seem outwardly similar to you – perhaps they live in the same area, or are the same age, or work or socialise with you – it's easy to assume that they are going to think in the same way as you do and make the same decisions as you would. But they might not. So don't give them the power and responsibility to make decisions that will affect your life. Wherever possible, make those decisions yourself.

Regard every rejection as motivation

Not everyone is going to think you're great. And not everyone is going to notice your fabulous qualities. But that's fine. Because every time you are rejected, or overlooked, or turned down, you can use the powerful surge of intense energy and anger you feel to motivate yourself to achieve even more. The phrase 'I'll show them' muttered fiercely under your breath is undoubtedly responsible for a very large number of achievements.

When Brian Acton was rejected for a job at Facebook in 2009, he didn't just go off and slump mournfully in front of the television for the rest of his life. Instead he tweeted: 'Looking forward to life's next adventure' and created WhatsApp, the instant phone-messaging app – which in a nice twist he sold to Facebook for US $19 billion five years later. That's some turnaround.

History is full of successful people who were rejected

the first time round and then used the power that rejection gave them to go on and become even more brilliant. Steven Spielberg was rejected twice by the University of Southern California's film school, because he did not have good enough grades. But this did not stop him becoming one of the most successful film-makers ever, making classic films such as *E.T.*, *Jaws* and *Jurassic Park*. Anna Wintour, the influential editor of US *Vogue*, was fired from her job as junior fashion editor at *Harper's Bazaar* for being 'too edgy'. Lady Gaga was dropped from her first music label. Marilyn Monroe was rejected by a modelling agency that advised her to try being a typist instead. Albert Einstein, the theoretical physicist, was expelled from high school for being a rebel and a dunce. He went on to devise the General Theory of Relativity, came up with the world's most famous equation $E = mc^2$ and in 1921 received the Nobel Prize for Physics. That really did show them.

NOW TAKE ACTION

1. If the gatekeepers of an industry continually reject you, consider how you might be able to do it anyway, on your own terms.

2. Look back at the rejections you have faced in your life. What happened next? Did the rejections inspire you to do better, think harder, run faster, be more creative in any way?

3. Look at the apps and websites you use – are they really providing you with a useful service or could you do it better yourself?

Chapter 9

Now add the magic ingredients

'The people who are crazy enough to think they can change the world are the ones who do'

Steve Jobs, inventor and entrepreneur

No matter what your key strengths are, there are a few special qualities that can make them work even more effectively. They are:

enthusiasm, imagination, optimism, ambition and determination

These are the magic ingredients that add sparkle to every situation. And the good news is that you already possess many of them. They may be buried, or underused, or hidden away; they may have been neglected for a while, but they are right there, inside you. They just need digging out, given a bit of a polish and some TLC, a bit of recognition for what they are and what they can be used for, and off you go. Let's take a look at each of them in turn.

Enthusiasm

Also known as: passion, energy, oomph

Enthusiasm is a lovely characteristic to have. It's a heady mix of sparkle, zest, zip and zing, a bouncy bubble of excitement and joy, and it's the quality that's going to carry you towards your goal even when nothing seems to be going your way.

Long before Jamie, Nigella, Marco and Gordon, there was Keith Floyd. The original celebrity chef, he first bounced onto our television screens in the 1980s, bursting with enthusiasm, energy and eccentricity, and a seemingly completely different way of looking at the world. Floyd broke all the rules of television, and indeed all the rules of cooking, throwing ingredients together, drinking a glass of wine, while chatting to an unseen cameraman and cooking in completely absurd locations, such as on a fishing boat in rough seas.

Things often didn't turn out as planned, but it didn't matter because Keith was so enthusiastic about what he was doing. His sheer energy and love of cooking would carry the show along and he was soon presenting his shows from locations around the world, endearing himself to millions of viewers with his gloriously chaotic, madcap style. He ended up making 23 television series and writing 19 cookbooks.

He summed up his approach in one of his books, saying, 'Cooking is an art and patience a virtue. Careful shopping, fresh ingredients and an unhurried approach are nearly all you need. There is one more thing – love. Love for food and love for those you invite to your table. With a combination of these things you can be an artist – not perhaps in the representational style of a Dutch master, but rather more like

Gauguin, the naive, or Van Gogh, the impressionist. Plates or pictures of sunshine taste of happiness and love.'

You too can be enthusiastic In fact you already know how to get enthusiastic about something, because you've done it many times before. Your first bicycle. Your eighth birthday party. Your new best friend. Your first holiday abroad. The only reason you might not be so enthusiastic these days is because you've forgotten where to look to find things that excite you and make you happy.

Imagination

Also known as: curiosity, creativity, innovation, invention

Imagination is a wonderfully exciting ingredient to have on board, because you never know where it might take you and what it might produce. What's more, having the ability to think up innovative solutions to problems can not only take you on an exhilarating ride, it can leave a lasting impact on other people's lives too.

Aron Gelbard was working for a management consultancy firm when he and Ben Stanway decided to start an online flower delivery business with a difference. Instead of sending the flowers in a bouquet and hoping that someone would be in to receive them, they decided to package the flowers in a box that fitted through a standard letterbox, so the deliveries could be made even if no one was at home.

When they discovered that some types of flower could be transported dry if they were kept flat, the two of them rented a room by the hour in London's New Covent Garden market to test out their idea, using their savings of a few thousand pounds to fund the venture. They would buy different types of flower and send them through the post in boxes to see whether they would arrive in good condition. While most varieties of flower coped well with the experience, others did not.

Aron says, 'In the early days we weren't sure if it was going to work. We sent free flowers to people and would go round to their houses to see what the flowers looked like when they arrived, and take photos and do surveys. We also went round different parts of London with a notepad and ruler measuring people's letterboxes to see how big the box needed to be.'

There were a few setbacks along the way. The prototype boxes they were using cost £30 each, so when the supplier told them that if they ordered a thousand boxes it would only cost them £2.70 per box, they jumped at the chance. They immediately placed an order for 1,000 boxes, and sent flowers to 20 people who had volunteered to trial the service. But when the flowers arrived many of them had mould on them because the boxes didn't have any ventilation holes.

Aron says, 'We had to throw away the other 980 boxes. What had seemed like a great saving actually turned out to be an expensive mistake.'

There was also a bad moment when the Royal Mail changed their pricing structure three weeks before the business launched. Aron says, 'For about a day we thought that the price of sending our flowers had trebled and that we would lose money on every order.' Fortunately, they discovered a different tariff, which was actually the one they should have been using in the first place, which made the numbers work.

They launched their business, Bloom & Wild (www.bloomandwild.com), in 2013 and now send out tens of thousands of boxes of flowers a month. Bloom & Wild has become the top-rated online flower company in the UK on review platforms and in 2017 the business, which employs 40 people, successfully raised a further £3.75 million in investment funding.

Now aged 34, Aron says, 'It is hard work but I have always believed in this. I feel incredibly fortunate. I love having a business that delivers happiness and a positive experience to people.'

You too can be imaginative It's easy to be as imaginative as a child because every day is full of new discoveries and new adventures. But as you get older you can lose the art of dreaming and of thinking up new ideas. That's partly because your job may not require that kind of skill and partly because the demands and responsibilities of everyday life squash down your imagination. But there is good news. Your imagination is not lost, it hasn't disappeared. It's just been lying dormant. It's still there inside you. You just need to find something to spark it off again.

Optimism

Also known as: positivity, hopefulness, self-belief, confidence

Optimists believe that things are going to turn out fine, and that in general good things will happen rather than bad things. They see any obstacles as temporary setbacks and failure as a mere blip on the road to success, rather than anything more permanent and final. They are also generally a lot more fun to be around.

One of them is Caitlin Moran. A columnist for *The Times* newspaper for 25 years, Caitlin is the oldest of eight children and was raised on benefits on a council estate in Wolverhampton. At the age of 11, she was taken out of school by her parents and educated herself at the library and by watching television. Somehow she discovered she could write well and won several writing competitions before having her first novel published when she was just 16. Caitlin became a music journalist for *Melody Maker* and, not long after, started writing regular columns for *The Times*. She has had five books published and co-wrote the Channel 4 sitcom *Raised by Wolves*.

When she was interviewed on Radio 4's *Desert Island Discs*, Caitlin said, 'I believe in giddy, deluded, intoxicated optimism because that is the fuel that will keep you going long after anger or righteousness or fear have burned out. I look everywhere for things to make me optimistic.'

Being optimistic is not just a lovely way to live life, it can be a key factor in achieving more too. A study of MBA graduates in 2010 by the US National Bureau of Economic Research discovered that the optimists found jobs more easily than the pessimists and were more likely to be promoted. By tracking the job-search performance and promotions of the students during the two years after they graduated, the authors of the report found the optimists achieved better outcomes, even though they had similar skills to the pessimists.

They said, 'During the job-search process, they spend less effort searching and are offered jobs more quickly. They are choosier and are more likely to be promoted than others. Although we find optimists are more charismatic and are perceived by others to be more likely to succeed, these factors alone do not explain away the findings. Most of the effect of optimism on economic outcomes stems from the part that is not readily observed by one's peers.'

You too can be optimistic You just have to believe that

good things can happen, and hold on to that feeling as tightly as you can. If you feel your optimism fading and diminishing as real life gets in the way, you can easily spruce it up. You just need to retrain the thoughts in your head.

Indeed Martin Seligman, a psychologist at the University of Pennsylvania, believes that we can learn optimism in the same way as many other skills. All it takes, he says, is to consciously challenge any negative self-talk. To prove his point he identified the more pessimistic students in his classes to participate in a study. The students were randomly split into two groups, with half of them asked to attend 16 hours of workshops on the techniques of learning optimism, and the other half acting as the control group and not attending any workshops at all.

After 18 months he assessed the two groups of students and discovered that while 29 per cent of the workshop participants suffered from depression and anxiety, that proportion rose to 47 per cent in the control group. The workshop participants also reported fewer general health problems over the period of the study than those in the control group.

Ambition

Also known as: focus, drive, mission

Ambition is the strong desire to achieve something. It's a pretty powerful ingredient – in fact I wrote my last book about it. People with a strong sense of ambition are highly likely to achieve more, simply because they are going to put all their effort and focus into making it happen.

When Lindsay Pattison, then the high-flying UK chief executive of Maxus, a global network of media agencies, was asked by a journalist from the *Guardian* newspaper what her next goal was, she immediately announced that she wanted her boss's job. Her comments caused quite a stir, with many people amazed that she had dared to express her ambition so boldly. Six months later, however, she did indeed get her boss's job and is now Global Chief Executive of Maxus, one of the most senior positions in the advertising world. In her new role she oversees 3,000 people in 55 countries and is responsible for spending more than £11.2 billion of media investment on behalf of clients.

She says, 'That interview has literally followed me around. Everyone always asks me about it. But why wouldn't I want my boss's job? I thought I could do it. What is so wrong with saying that? I always want to improve, learn more, and achieve more. So that means a different job, and yes, a bigger job. I don't like standing still so when you take a new job it should be a big leap ahead of what you think you can possibly do, because that is when you dive in and learn loads.'

She adds, 'I think saying out loud what your ambition is, does truly help. It is good to test it out and see how it sounds and feels, then you can work on an effective frequency to ensure you are heard.'

Lindsay thinks that much of her drive and desire to win comes from the fact she was a competitive swimmer as a child and even trialled for the Olympic Games. The youngest of four children, she joined a swimming club with her siblings at the age of four and began competing from the age of six. She would train two or three mornings a week before school and two evenings, and compete in swimming competitions every weekend. By the age of 14, she was the best swimmer for her age in her county.

She says, 'Competitive swimming taught me that there is a direct correlation between the effort you put into something and what you get out. The harder you train, the better your rewards are.'

You too can be ambitious You have big goals. You have somewhere fabulous you want to get to. After all, that's why you are reading this book. People get scared of the word ambition, but it is simply the desire to achieve more in life. Ambition is a great thing to have on board because it will make the journey to success so much easier. Embrace it and be pleased you've got it.

Determination

Also known as: tenacity, perseverance, persistence, resilience

Determination is a wonderful ingredient for getting things done. Having the ability to persevere and persist at trying to achieve your goal is going to give you a much better chance of actually achieving it.

James Dyson was running his own company selling a plastic wheelbarrow he had designed when one day he became so frustrated with the poor performance of a vacuum cleaner he had bought that he took it apart. He discovered that its bag was clogged with dust, which had caused the suction to drop, and so he decided to create a vacuum cleaner that does not lose suction. His big idea was to get rid of the bag altogether and replace it with a fast-spinning motor that creates a cyclone of air to suck the carpet clean. He made a prototype, but it didn't work. So he made another, and then another. Neither of them worked either, but by now James was determined not to give up. He ended up spending the next five years making and testing prototypes.

He told one magazine, 'There are countless times an inventor can give up on an idea. By the time I made my fifteenth prototype, my third child was born. By prototype 2,627, my wife and I were really counting our pennies. By 3,727, my wife was giving art lessons for some extra cash. These were tough times, but each failure brought me closer to solving the problem.'

In the end James had to make 5,127 prototypes before he was able to come up with a model that worked. But even though he had successfully created his product, his problems were only just beginning. He couldn't find anyone in the UK who was willing to manufacture his new cleaner because they didn't want to affect their lucrative sales of vacuum-cleaner replacement bags. So in 1993 he set up a factory to manufacture his cleaner himself, a huge risk because he had to borrow a large amount of money against his house to pay for it. But the gamble paid off and two years later his Dual Cyclone model had become the bestselling cleaner in the UK.

James created other versions of his cleaner and by 2005 his Dyson cleaners had become the market leader in the USA and he was able to launch a range of other products, including hand dryers and fans. His business now employs more than 7,000 people worldwide, and is hugely profitable. In 2015 it had revenues of £1.74 billion and made a profit of £448 million.

James has said that the most important trait of an inventor is 'doggedness', explaining, 'I have always found that the very moment you're ready to give up, that if you go on a little longer, you end up finding what you're looking for. It's one of life's rewards for perseverance.'

You too can be determined In fact you already are. Remember that running race that no one thought you would win? Or that exam that everyone presumed you would fail? Or maybe you're left handed and have had to constantly battle to use household items made for those who are right handed: scissors, knives, tin openers, anything with an electric cord. You may not notice it, but every day you are fighting and winning small battles that test your resilience and prove your determination. So take heart – you've already got what it takes.

NOW TAKE ACTION

1. Start thinking of ways to get your imagination firing again. Start reading books you might not normally read – you could even start an informal book club with some friends so you have the opportunity to discuss what you are reading with others.

2. Make a list of the leisure activities you love doing. It might be going camping, ice-skating, playing tennis, rowing a boat across a lake. Now write down the date when you last did any of these things. The answer may shock you. Now find out if you can do any of these locally and do one of them next weekend.

3. Think about the tough times in your life, when you have had to show determination and resilience to get through the experience. How well did you cope? What got you through?

Chapter 10

Take the first step

'Life can only be understood backwards;
but it must be lived forwards'

Søren Kierkegaard, philosopher

There's a lovely concept in physics called momentum, which describes the tendency of a moving object to keep moving in the same direction. Basically, the more momentum a moving object has, the harder it is to stop it. It's a lovely thought, the idea that by moving forward, you are making it easier for you to move forward, and that once you have got going, you can just keep going. And it's a pretty handy concept to apply to the idea of achieving more: if you can launch yourself in the right direction, even with the smallest of nudges, then the momentum you generate will make it easier to keep going than to stop.

This is how to do it.

Start the ball rolling

If you can take the first step, no matter how small that step is, then you immediately change the status of something from impossible to possible. And that changes everything.

Kathryn Joosten was a divorced single mother bringing up her two young children on her own, taking on three part-time jobs to make ends meet. She had very little time to herself and no time at all to think about what she really wanted to do with her life. Then one day at the age of 42 she took part in a local amateur dramatics production and realised she loved acting and would really like to pursue it as a career. But with children to support, taking any kind of big leap into show business was out of the question.

Instead of giving up on her dream, however, she decided to keep plugging away at it and take it one step at a time. So she initially performed in more amateur productions to gain experience, then when her sons were ten and 12, she asked them if they would let her spend a year putting all her energy and free time into trying to achieve some kind of success as an actress. They agreed, so she moved from doing community theatre to semi-professional theatre, and eventually she got a job as a street performer in Disney's Hollywood theme park in Orlando.

She spent another two years doing local theatre, then when her sons left home she decided to try her luck in Los Angeles for six months. By now, however, she was in her mid-fifties. She didn't have an agent, she didn't have any contacts in the industry, and she didn't have any kind of track record that was likely to impress a Hollywood casting director.

But she went to every audition she could and eventually after five months she got her first television job, a two-line part in the sitcom *Family Matters*. That led to other parts in *ER* and *Roseanne*, and kickstarted a fantastic acting career in television, including playing the President's secretary in *The West Wing* and Mrs McCluskey in *Desperate Housewives*, for which Kathryn won two Emmys.

She said, 'I didn't start out saying, "Gee, I think I'll try to win an Emmy." I just kept aiming down the path that seemed to shine before me. Each step I took was a natural progression, and I always arranged that I could go back and resume my previous life if I didn't get to the next step.'

Her determination to give it a go was inspired by her mother, who died of cancer at the age of 49. Kathryn explained, 'She spent her last months bitterly regretting that she had deferred so many dreams, which now would never be fulfilled. It impressed me deeply, and I had vowed that I would never let that happen to me.'

Kickstart your curiosity

The château at Clos Lucé (www.vinci-closluce.com) in France's Loire Valley, is an extraordinary place. It is now a museum and has gardens that are full of wonderful wooden models of machines, such as a paddle wheel, a two-level bridge and a water mill. The château itself is filled with dozens of detailed scientific diagrams and drawings from the fifteenth century showing the inventions of the parachute, helicopter, bicycle and tank, some 500 years ahead of their time.

Incredibly, all these things are the work of one man, Leonardo da Vinci, who spent the last few years of his life at Clos Lucé after being invited to stay there by the King of France. Even more incredibly, the artefacts represent a tiny

KNOWHOW

Museums often hold events and discussions that you can take part in – four times a year the National Museum of Science and Media in Bradford (www. scienceandmediamuseum.org.uk), for example, holds special 'Lates' events in the evening for adults only. These are free three-hour events that may include live experiments and exclusive talks. Find the museums nearest to you, then go online and sign up for their newsletters to keep informed about what is going on.

fraction of his life's work, which also included the *Mona Lisa*, perhaps the most famous painting of all time, and his drawing of *Vitruvian Man*, now regarded as a cultural icon. The official website dedicated to him describes Leonardo as scientist, mathematician, engineer, inventor, anatomist, painter, sculptor, architect, botanist, musician and writer.

Leonardo da Vinci's boundless energy came from his relentless curiosity about the world and how it worked. He said, 'The noblest pleasure is the joy of understanding' and 'It had long since come to my attention that people of accomplishment rarely sat back and let things happen to them. They went out and happened to things.'

You too can follow your curiosity and see where it leads. Make the effort to find out more about the things that interest you. It may take you to places, people, events, courses and even to a whole new career.

Start asking yourself questions about the world. Why, how, who, what? Why not, why so, why now? Don't just watch the news headlines, start following interesting people on Twitter and read the articles they share, borrow books you would never normally think of reading from the library, strike up conversations with interesting people. The more you start wondering about things, the more your imagination will start firing up, and the more ideas will flow.

Identify your audience

Whatever you are trying to do, and regardless of whether it is particularly creative or not, you need to try and find an audience. That is, a group of people who are interested in what you are doing and want to hear more; and ideally who will keep on being interested in what you are doing as you progress. If you are starting out as a photographer, for example, these will be the people who like your work and buy it. If you are starting a business, it will be your customers. If you're a performer, it will be the people who buy tickets to see you on stage.

Everyone needs an audience. Not just because their interest translates into money to fund your work and makes it possible for you to do interesting things, but because having an appreciative audience gives you energy, enthusiasm, inspiration and motivation like nothing else can.

I've taken two solo shows to the Edinburgh Fringe Festival, once in 2010 to do 13 performances and again in 2016 to do 24 performances. The number of people attending my show varied hugely day to day, as it does for every Edinburgh Fringe show, meaning that I sometimes found myself performing my show to an audience of more than 50 people, sometimes to 20 or 30 people, and once, memorably, to an audience of two people. I can tell you now, it is a lot easier to find the energy and buzz in a room when there are 50 other people in it, all laughing and smiling and clapping, than when there are two.

Think about who your audience might be, what kind of people they are, and how you might reach them. That might mean starting a Facebook page, holding a local event in your neighbourhood, creating a blog or even writing a book. If you are saying or doing something interesting, you also need to find the people who would be interested in hearing it.

Set something different in motion – today

The theoretical physicist Albert Einstein defined insanity as doing the same thing over and over again and expecting different results. It's a brilliant statement and it makes a lot of sense. So why not change one thing about your life or work right now and see what happens.

Here are three random ideas to get you started:

1. Change the scenery

There's nothing like a dramatic change of scene to get the ideas flowing. If you live in the city why not pack your walking shoes and take a train to the countryside – or even another country. Eurostar (www.eurostar.co.uk), for example, has started running direct trains from London to Avignon and Marseille in the south of France. It takes five hours and they sometimes offer special one-way fares for £49. Or if you live in a rural area, get into the city for inspiration – cities like Bath, Oxford and Edinburgh have amazing old buildings and a real sense of history and heritage. Hop on a bus once you are there to get your bearings before setting out on foot with a guidebook.

2. Apply to be a magistrate

Magistrates are part-time volunteers who hear cases in courts in their community. You don't need formal qualifications or legal training, but you do need to be of good character and to be able to sit and concentrate for long periods of time. You can be any age between 18 and 65 and you will be given full training for the role, and a legal adviser in court will help you with questions about the law. You can find out more and download an application form at Gov.uk (www.gov.uk).

3. Do something fun this summer

If you've never spent the summer working on a French campsite, it's time to remedy that right now and become a holiday courier, as they are known. You won't get paid a huge amount and it can be hard work, but you will discover all kinds of skills you never knew you had, from putting up tents, to being resourceful and talking to customers. There is no age limit and you can even apply to do the job with a friend or partner. Try Canvas Holidays (www.canvasholidays.co.uk), Eurocamp (www.eurocamp.co.uk) and Al Fresco (www.alfresco-holidays.com), all of which employ couriers of all ages, or check out the Season Workers (www.seasonworkers.com) website.

Keep the flame burning

If you can't commit to your goal full time, or even most of the time right now, you need to make sure that you keep it alive and breathing. Even if you can do only tiny little bits, here and there, do them. If you keep doing small amounts, then eventually your project will get its own momentum and carry you along with it.

When I visited my friend Julie in New York for the first time, I was astonished to discover that everyone I met there seemed to have all these interesting creative projects that they were working on in their spare time. Screenplays, novels, dotcom start-ups, photography, dog training, clothes design, cooking, an endless list of determined endeavour. It was really inspiring, and exciting – the idea that you didn't have to be defined by the job you did for money; instead you could choose to define yourself by the projects you did.

But these projects were not to be confused with hobbies; people weren't doing them just for fun, they were doing them with a real purpose in mind. That purpose was that, hopefully, one day the projects would become substantial enough that something amazing might spring from them – a better job, some money, a better way to live. Those people were undertaking their projects with one eye on the future.

Put up some signposts

It can be very useful to erect some signposts to keep you moving in the right direction. That might be arranging a regular chat with a supportive person in your life, or it might be making a regular visit to a place that you find inspiring. It might be dipping into a favourite book on a regular basis to remind you of its most useful insights, or doing a high-intensity sport that reminds you how good it feels to perform at your best.

Ian Haworth has a high-flying career in advertising, as the executive creative director for the UK, the Middle East, Europe and Africa for Wunderman, part of the global agency WPP. He also swims six times a week in the unheated Serpentine Lake in London, going there every morning before work, all year round, no matter what the weather. It may be dark, raining and freezing cold, even to the extent of having to break the ice before he gets in the water, but Ian will still swim – and only in trunks, not a wetsuit. And he believes there is a very strong connection between the extreme swimming and his success at work.

He says, 'Swimming like this drives me really hard and challenges me mentally. It gives me a lot more energy, and ability to focus and it helps me do things that I didn't think I could ever do. It also gives me a real tranquillity and incredible calmness, because I know that whatever else I am going to do in my day, isn't going to be as hard. This morning it was 3 degrees in the water and the other day it was so dark I swam into a swan and woke it up.'

Ian, who is now 57, adds, 'Doing some kind of extreme sport has always helped me to push myself physically to see how far I can go, and that has enabled me to really push myself at work and try and make the most of what I have got. The byproduct is I can achieve more.'

Don't limit yourself

Don't place a limit on how far you think you can go, or where you think you could get to. Other factors may eventually limit your journey, but that factor should not be you. Your job is simply to face the right direction and start moving.

When New York advertising agency We Believers suggested to Salt Water Brewery in Florida that they make an edible version of the plastic rings that are used to hold six-packs of beer together, it was intended purely as a marketing gimmick. The craft brewer made some rings from wheat and barley left over from the brewing process as a fun way to promote their beer.

But both firms quickly realised that they had accidentally hit upon a real need, because the plastic rings used to keep beer cans together in packs have become a significant environmental problem. They often end up in the ocean where they trap and strangle wildlife and get swallowed by marine animals. It is estimated that a million seabirds and 100,000 marine animals, including sea turtles, around the world die every year after becoming trapped in the plastic rings or eating them.

So the agency and the brewery have now created a spin-off company together to manufacture the edible pack rings for real. The rings, which they have called E6PR, are both edible and 100 per cent biodegradable. They start to break up within two hours of being in the ocean, and yet are every bit as efficient at holding cans together as the plastic version. As they are made from byproducts of the brewing process, they are environmentally friendly in that way too. The joint-venture company has now found a factory to mass produce the rings and is in the process of exploring deals with bigger beer companies with the aim of making edible rings the new industry standard. Indeed, the firm now hopes the edible six-pack rings will be the start of a worldwide movement to rid the packaging industry of plastic altogether.

NOW TAKE ACTION

1. Make today your start date. If you'd like to mark the
    occasion in some way, you can:
    email me at rachel@rachelbridge.com
    or tweet me @rachelbridge100
    and I will send you lots of best wishes.

2. Consider who your audience might be and how you
    might go about communicating with it.

3. Think about a signpost that you can put up in your
    life to help you stay on track.

———————————

Chapter 11

Keep it real

'Keep your eyes on the stars, but remember
to keep your feet on the ground'

Theodore Roosevelt, American President

I love the word pragmatic. I think it might actually be my favourite word. I use it all the time. It perhaps best sums up the way I see life and how to approach it. Now, the word pragmatic is not a cool or fashionable word. According to the dictionary it means 'dealing with things sensibly and realistically in a way that is based on practical rather than theoretical considerations'. It also gets a bad press in the thesaurus, which offers synonyms for it such as logical, practical, realistic, efficient, down to earth, matter of fact, unidealistic. The exact opposite, you might think, of achieving your hopes and dreams.

But here's the thing. It is by being logical, practical and realistic that you have the very best chance of actually achieving your dreams. That's because this down-to-earth approach helps you see very clearly what is possible, what is not possible and what might just be possible with a dollop of hard work and an ounce or two of luck. It's about seeing what you've got, getting excited at its potential and its possibilities, and then rolling up your sleeves and getting on with it.

Dreams and ideas are a great place to start, but if you really want to make them happen, you need to anchor them in real life, in your life, by knowing and using your strengths in the most effective ways. As the writer Aldous Huxley once said, 'Dream in a pragmatic way.'

Here are some ways to do this:

Get the basics in place

Whenever you have a big, exciting idea, immediately start pegging it down with practical details before it floats off. How will you actually do this? What will you need to organise? What information do you need? How much will it cost? The more you can get the practical elements in place, the more likely you are to be able to turn your ideas into reality.

Not long ago a lady got in touch with me via Twitter because she wanted to talk to me about an idea she had for a television show. She was full of enthusiasm and excitement about how it would work and how she thought I might get involved. She had also come up with a brand name to describe herself and what she did, which she could use for the show. It was a really good name and she couldn't wait to start pitching her idea to television producers.

When I asked her what she had done to protect this name to stop anyone else from using it, however, it turned out that she hadn't done anything at all. She hadn't trademarked the name and she hadn't bought the domain name for a website, or any variations. She hadn't even registered the name on any social media sites. She had got so caught up in the excitement of thinking about her television show that she had completely failed to deal with any of the basic practicalities. About half way through our conversation it finally dawned on her just how vital all this was and she quickly cut short our chat so that she could rush off and secure her brand name before anyone else did.

KNOWHOW

You should start pinning your idea down too. Go online and buy any website domain names you will need. LCN (www.lcn.com) and GoDaddy (www.godaddy.com) are good places to start. Set up any social media accounts you will need on Twitter, Facebook, Instagram, Pinterest and YouTube.

If you think you may need to trademark a name or register a design, check out the Intellectual Property Office website (www.ipo.gov.uk). Trademarks cost from £200 upwards and you can apply for them online.

You can check whether a business in the UK has already taken the name you want on the Companies House website (www.companieshouse.gov.uk). It's free to do this.

Be flexible

While it may feel terribly exciting and dramatic to be an all-or-nothing kind of person, it doesn't achieve much. Understanding in a very unemotional and clear-eyed way what you can and can't do is a much more productive way to achieve your dreams.

It may be that you don't have the talent, or the resources, or skills, or money to do exactly as you had planned. But it might still be possible to make a few small changes until the outcome is just as good. Perhaps you can't be the next Jeremy Clarkson, paid huge amounts by the BBC and Amazon to drive around in fast cars all day. But you can still be a car designer, or engineer, or mechanic, or the organiser of car shows, or a hundred other things to do with cars.

The secret is to have a real understanding and awareness of where your true strengths lie, and what resources you have, and then to adapt and tweak your idea until it matches what you are capable of doing.

If you dream of running a bar in Spain, for example, but lack the money or freedom to be able to simply abandon your old life to go out to Spain and buy a bar, don't give up on the whole idea. Instead, work out what exactly it is that appeals to you so much about the goal you have. Is it the thought of being in Spain that excites you, for example, or the thought of running a bar? Or is it the idea of being your own boss, or having your own business, or the chance to meet new people, or live in a place where the sun always shines? Now ask yourself – would you be just as happy running a bar somewhere else? Or being in Spain doing something else? Or working for someone else running a bar in Spain? Or working for yourself and meeting lots of new people each day? Or doing anything, anywhere, as long as it's hot and you are by the sea? Because any one of these options could be just as much fun, and perhaps a lot more feasible financially and logistically.

Accept that you may need to start at the bottom

Just because you decide you want to do something doesn't mean that the world is suddenly going to say, 'Yes, of course, how wonderful, please step this way.' You may need to work your way up to the place where you want to be.

I once knew a lawyer who was unhappy in his job. He realised he'd chosen the wrong career and had decided that he wanted to be a journalist instead. He asked me for some advice so I arranged to meet him for a drink to have a chat.

I started advising him about how he might be able to get a job as a reporter on a weekly or monthly trade magazine, particularly one that was about the legal profession, as he would be able to show some knowledge and experience, and then how he could start from there and gradually work his way up.

But he quickly interrupted me and said airily, 'Oh, I don't want to be a journalist on a trade magazine. I only want to write for *The Times*.'

But why would *The Times* want to employ a former lawyer without any experience of being a journalist? Journalism is like any other trade – you have to start at the bottom, learn how to do it and work your way up. You can't just jump into the best bits simply because you rather like the idea of it. It doesn't work like that.

I tried to explain all this to him, but he just didn't want to know. So I left him to his unrealistic dreams and changed the subject. The last time I heard of him, he was still being a lawyer.

Be prepared to find a Plan B – or a Plan C

Sometimes you really can't get what you want, perhaps because you don't have what it takes, or because circumstances conspire against you, or for a dozen other reasons.

It can be hard to accept that sometimes doors that slam shut in your face stay shut. But this is the point where you get to show what you are really made of. You can either collapse in a heap, go home and hide under the duvet and never attempt anything ever again, or you can dust yourself down and get to work tackling plan B. Remember, you have resilience.

When he was growing up, Gordon Ramsay wanted to be a professional footballer. At the age of 12, he was selected for the Warwickshire under-14 team, then when he was 18 he trialled with Glasgow Rangers for their youth team. He trained with them for a few months, but when he seriously injured his knee, smashing the cartilage, his dreams of becoming a professional footballer were dashed forever.

It was a massive disappointment, but rather than dwelling on what could never be, Gordon decided to try and achieve success in a completely different area. He enrolled at North Oxfordshire Technical College to study hotel management and then began working in restaurant kitchens as a commis chef, gradually working his way up to head chef of La Tante Claire in London. He is now one of the best-known chefs in the world, with his signature restaurant, Restaurant Gordon Ramsay in Chelsea, holding three Michelin stars since 2001. He has been the star of several reality television shows, owns many restaurants and has amassed a personal fortune of US $175 million, according to *Forbes* Rich List. He has achieved the success he dreamed of, just in a completely different area to the one he initially imagined.

Embrace your restrictions

Too much choice can sometimes be overwhelming. If every aspect of your life is up for grabs, then it can be hard to know where to start making changes. Sometimes it can actually be helpful to have some fixed, immoveable boundaries already in place.

You may be restricted in where you can live, for example, perhaps because you need to live close to elderly parents, or because your children are at a school they love. But that's okay. Stop seeing the restriction as a problem and start counting it as a blessing, because it is one less thing for you to have to make a decision about.

Geoff Dyer addresses this issue in a typically robust and amusing way in his book *Out of Sheer Rage*. Geoff is supposed to be writing either a book about D. H. Lawrence, or a novel, but is stuck on both. He writes, 'One of the reasons, in fact, that it was impossible to get started on either the Lawrence book or the novel was because I was so preoccupied with where to live. I could have lived anywhere, all I had to do was choose – but it was impossible to choose because I could live anywhere. There were no constraints on me and because of this it was impossible to choose. It's easy to make choices where you have things hampering you – a job, kids' schools – but when all you have to go on is your own desires, then life becomes considerably more difficult, not to say intolerable.'

Stop being annoyed about the parts of your life you cannot change, and concentrate all your efforts on the bits you can.

Stay clear-eyed

The more honestly you can assess your current situation as it really is, the faster you will be able to see what elements of it you can turn to your advantage. One of the most unpleasant experiences of modern working life is being made redundant. If not handled in the right way, it can seriously shatter your confidence and ability to look forward. Yet according to a survey of small firms by specialist insurer Hiscox, 17 per cent of the start-up businesses in the UK were launched because the founder was made redundant from his or her previous job. It might not have been how they had planned it, but who cares? They've now got their own businesses.

If you can start seeing things as they are and not as you would like them to be, you can make the best of any situation.

Work with what you've got

Journalist Rosie Millard and her husband Pip, a television producer, reached a point in their lives at which they realised they really wanted to go on a big round-the-world adventure. But they had four young children and they knew they didn't want to either leave them behind, or disrupt their schooling or uproot them from their home and friends by taking them away for too long. So they kept it short, packed a lot in and did their big round-the-world adventure largely during the school summer holidays.

In that time they visited six French overseas domains, including Martinique, Guyane and French Polynesia. They saw some amazing things, had wonderful experiences together as a family, and even made a television documentary series about the places they visited. Rosie also wrote a book about the trip, called *Bonnes Vacances*. Because of the way they timed it, the children missed hardly any school, and very few of the other activities they loved doing, such as going to Brownies, playing team sports and learning to play musical instruments.

Rosie says, 'You don't have to go for a year. You can get the same effect going away for a shorter amount of time, and you don't have to totally wreck your life in doing it. We had the most amazing experiences and an extraordinary adventure, and the impact on the children was enormous. It was a major bonding experience and was something that we all shared.'

She adds: 'Because we hadn't taken them away for that long, they just slotted back into their schools when we came back and everything just carried on as normal. The trip enhanced their lives without destabilising them, and I think that was important.'

Understand that success comes on its own terms

It would be lovely to be able to control exactly how and when you achieve your goals, but no matter how much you might want to, in reality you don't get to choose. Even if you picked what you intended to be the direct route, success is not something you can nail down like that. It happens when it happens and the best you can do is make sure you are pointing in the right direction, aiming for where you want to go, and that you are ready to deal with whatever happens along the way.

Don't panic if success doesn't come to you in a straight line, either, with every achievement leading smoothly on to the next. Success doesn't work like that. It's not linear. It curves and goes up and down and curls back on itself. That project you're working on might turn out to be a soaring arc, or a loop, or a dead end. Just because one thing you did was a success doesn't mean the next thing will be too. But equally, the thing after that could be even more amazing than you'd hoped. And meanwhile along the way you will have learnt something from everything you did – even the parts that didn't turn out the way you imagined.

And don't worry if success is not immediate. Everyone loves the idea of overnight success. Journalists in particular adore it because it makes for such good stories. But there is no such thing. It's a myth. Look behind the headlines and you will find that every single person who is celebrated as an overnight success has actually put in many years of effort and toil getting to that point. As footballing legend Lionel Messi put it in an advert he did for Adidas, 'I start early and I stay late, day after day, year after year. It took me 17 years and 114 days to become an overnight success.'

Set yourself a realistic timetable, be patient and don't underestimate how long things are going to take. Yes, you are impatient to get to where you want to be, of course you are, but if you expect everything to happen exactly when you want it to, you are likely to be disappointed. Allow yourself time to achieve something brilliant. As the saying goes, Rome wasn't built in a day.

NOW TAKE ACTION

1. Start training yourself to find the opportunity in every situation, no matter how negative it initially appears. Your train has been cancelled? Take the opportunity to explore a different way of getting to work. The gym is closed for refurbishment? Take the opportunity to try out a different type of exercise.

2. If you think there is a chance that you could be made redundant at work, start preparing now for what you will do next. You will immediately feel a lot more confident and in control of the situation. Get your CV ready, strengthen your network of useful contacts, calculate how much redundancy money you might receive, if any. And above all, start thinking about what exciting things you could do next.

3. Start being kinder to yourself. Don't spend all your time trying to be the person you think you ought to be, when you could be making the most of being the person you really are. You may love the idea of being the kind of person who goes to three-day music festivals, or invites everyone round for big Sunday lunches. But if you loathe the thought of camping in a muddy field and can't stand cooking, then stop tying yourself in knots and make the most of being you.

———————

Chapter 12

Start getting excited

*'You must expect great things of yourself
before you can do them'*

Michael Jordan, basketball player

Now that you can see how much you could achieve by playing to your strengths, it's time to start getting excited. That's because there is a whole world of possibilities out there and it's all within your grasp. Which means that your new life, whether at work or at home, or both, is just a step away.

Here are some of the things you could be doing:

You could have an adventure

The best ideas don't involve filling in an application form – they simply require the realisation that amazing experiences are just out there waiting for you to grab them. When Dick Kempson retired from his job as a teacher at the age of 60, he decided to mark the occasion by walking from his home in

Canterbury to Rome. He didn't do any kind of grand fitness preparation in advance – he simply walked to Dover, caught the ferry to France, and started walking in the general direction of Italy. His wife accompanied him for some of the way, but mostly he walked on his own, setting off early each morning and booking small hotels as he went.

Dick says, 'I wasn't a quick walker, I wasn't fit or strong, but I would get up each day and walk and keep going.'

Indeed, he became so absorbed in doing the walk for its own sake that halfway through France he abandoned the daily blog he had been trying to write, signing off with the words: 'There is nothing to say. I am, thankfully, delightedly, too busy just being. It is the walk that's the thing, doing it, not thinking about it. And that has brought me the deepest of pleasures and satisfactions.'

Dick eventually reached Rome three months after he had started out from home. He says, 'It was an absolutely extraordinary experience. It was totally worth doing. I had set myself a goal that was way beyond what I thought might be achievable, and yet it was utterly achievable, by just getting up and doing that day's contribution towards it. It gives me the conviction that I can do anything, and that the limit in most of our lives is not that we are too ambitious, it is that we are not ambitious enough. My walk to Rome stands there saying to me, you can set any goal in front of you; all you have to do is create a programme of how you are going to get there and follow it.'

You could be a pioneer

A great way to show what you are made of is to do something that has rarely been attempted before. That doesn't mean you have to trek across a remote jungle. Closer to home it could mean entering a profession that is just opening up to you. Right now only one per cent of the people working in the building and construction industry are women, and only one in every thousand electrical contractors are female, and there's no real reason for this other than a historical one. Two support networks have been set up to help women get into these professions and progress through them – Women on the Tools (www.womenonthetools.org.uk) provides advice and support for those seeking to forge a career in the construction industry, while the electrical body NICEIC runs a Jobs for the Girls campaign (www.niceic.com/jobsforthegirls), which offers mentoring, events and advice for women looking to get into the electrical trade.

You could learn a new skill

If you've ever wanted to play a musical instrument it's never too late to start. The orchestra practising in the rehearsal room in Bow in East London every Saturday morning is full of enthusiastic beginners, many of whom have never played an instrument before and can't read music. But this is no youth orchestra. This is the East London Late Starters Orchestra (www.ellso.org), which was set up in 1982 to provide an opportunity for people in middle age and beyond to learn a musical instrument and experience the enjoyment of playing as part of a group. No auditions are needed to join the orchestra and people are welcome regardless of their age, background and experience.

The orchestra came about after the council, which ran a weekly music group for children, arranged a drop-in session for parents to see what their children would be doing. The parents had a go, loved it and realised they wanted to keep on playing. As one of the players says on the orchestra's website, 'I had a preliminary lesson on the cello and I thought, "This is amazing!" I could learn to play these instruments. It was just such an incredible moment.'

Find out if there is anything like this in your area – and if there isn't, get in touch with some local music teachers and consider starting up one yourself.

You could be a great leader

If you have never considered being the leader of anything, you could be just the sort of person who is very good at it. The best leaders are not super-confident, arrogant, loud and ego-driven; they are thoughtful, empathetic, inclusive, accessible and inspiring, and very good at listening.

According to a survey of 189,000 business leaders in 81 organisations around the world by consulting firm McKinsey, the four most effective leadership traits are the ability to be supportive, to seek out different perspectives, to be focused on achieving results and to solve problems effectively.

Almost every walk of life needs good leaders to guide and direct and inspire people, from leading a campaign to organising a charity walk. A good place to start is in your local community – the Scouts (www.scouts.org.uk) and Girl Guides (www.girlguiding.org.uk), for example, are always looking for people interested in becoming volunteer leaders – find out more on their websites.

You could make a difference

Blake Mycoskie was travelling through Argentina in 2006 when he befriended some children in a village and discovered they had no shoes. So he started a business, TOMS (www.toms.co.uk), which gives a pair of new shoes to a needy child for every pair of shoes it sells.

The idea has worked so well that TOMS has expanded into other ways of helping people in need. For every pair of sunglasses it sells, it provides an eye examination for a person in need, as well as prescription glasses, sight-saving surgery or some other medical treatment. For every bag of coffee it sells, it provides a week's worth of safe drinking water to a person in need. And for every bag it sells, it provides the materials and training to help a woman give birth safely. TOMS has now given more than 75 million pairs of shoes to children in need in more than 70 countries around the world and restored sight to more than 400,000 people.

You too could make a difference, in all kinds of different ways. Check out the TOMS website for inspiration.

You could try something completely different

If you have already had a career but would love to use your skills in a very different way, you could retrain as a teacher. Secondary schools in particular are crying out for enthusiastic teachers. The organisation NowTeach (www.nowteach.org.uk) has been co-founded by former *Financial Times* journalist Lucy Kellaway to help people retrain as maths, science and language teachers for challenging London secondary schools. Alternatively, check out the Get into Teaching website (www.getintoteaching.education.gov.uk) for details of other routes into the profession. If you've already got a degree and would like to teach a priority subject, for example, you may be eligible for a bursary or scholarship of up to £25,000.

You could do something that matters to you

You get one shot at life so it makes sense to focus your energy and effort on doing something you feel is really worthwhile. Elaine Coomber used to earn a fortune working in the private equity department of a London bank and had a glamorous lifestyle to match. But despite the good salary she felt there was something missing in her life. She realised she envied her friends who had become doctors, so when she returned to the workplace after having two children she decided to retrain as a doctor herself. It was an enormous decision to take – she was 32, her children were just two and three years old, and she didn't even have the right A levels to study medicine.

She says, 'Everyone thought I was mad to consider it. I knew it would not be an easy route to take and all my friends advised me not to do it. So I explored every possible thing I could, to see if there was something in the medical field I could do that wasn't quite as hard as medicine would be. But after two years of soul searching I knew I had to try and become a doctor because I didn't want to be fifty and look back with regret. That was the biggest motivator.'

Elaine managed to get a place on an Access to Medicine course, an intensive one-year course for people who want to become doctors, but don't have the necessary A Levels. With the help of her mother, who drove over every morning to look after her children and take them to nursery, Elaine was able to take up the place and the following year she got a place at Brighton Medical School. She studied there for five years, before working as a junior doctor for another four years, all the time juggling long working hours with raising her children. She then worked as a GP trainee for another three years.

Elaine finally completed her medical training in 2016 at the age of 47, 13 years after she started down this path. She now works in the A&E department at Exeter Hospital and earns a fraction of what she did in the City working for a bank. But she knows she made the right choice. She says, 'I am very glad I did it. It feels right. I get real pleasure from dealing with patients. Just holding their hands and talking to them makes you feel that you are improving things for them, even in a little way. I would always have regretted not doing this, and now I have a purpose and a career, which I really enjoy and get enormous fulfilment from. It has given me a different perspective on life and I am very happy.'

KNOWHOW

Some medical schools offer medicine foundation courses which are designed as a route for learners with a good academic record in non-science subjects. You can find a list of UK medical schools offering foundation courses on the Get Into Medicine website (www.getintomedicine.co.uk).

You could stand out from the crowd

You don't have to conform to someone else's idea of what a brilliant life looks like; you can make up your own version. Amazing things can happen when you decide to do things a bit differently and ask, 'What happens if I try it this way, or that way?'

If you want to see something extraordinary, take a look at the website of Lings Cars (www.lingscars.com). It is a hectic cluttered cacophony of flashing graphics, neon colours, click-through buttons, music and noise. It has quizzes and games and every one of the Frequently Asked Questions is answered with a shaky video of a crazy air hostess, sometimes swigging from a bottle of whisky.

However, there is method behind the madness. Lings Cars was created by Ling Valentine, a Chinese immigrant who arrived in the UK by way of Finland, where she met her husband John while studying for a master's degree. Her husband had set up a car-leasing business and so she learnt the business from him and took over running it herself.

And while her website is never going to win any design awards, it has certainly got Ling and her business noticed. A few years ago she was invited to appear on the show *Dragons' Den*, where she was offered investment which she turned down, and she is now often asked to speak at events. Having begun running the business from home, Lings Cars now has an office in Gateshead and a staff of ten.

As Ling says on her website, 'Don't be deceived . . . I may be a scruffy Chinese girl, but I have more happy new-car customers and supply more new cars than many of the anonymous (and some big-name) leasing companies out there, combined.'

NOW TAKE ACTION

1. How can you get yourself noticed by the people or influencers who could help you carve out your better life? Could you make a speech at an event they will be attending? Or write an article for a magazine they will read?

2. Look back at what you have achieved so far in life. What achievements are you most proud of?

3. What charities inspire you? Write a list of three of them and then identify ways in which you can make a contribution other than a simple donation.

———————

Chapter 13

Ten powerful ideas to help you on your way

'You only live once, but if you do it right, once is enough'

Mae West, actress

I f you've spent years thinking that you don't have what it takes to be a success, it can be astonishing to realise that you do have everything you need, after all. Getting into this new way of thinking can, however, feel strange initially. As you start to make the most of the qualities and strengths you have, here are ten important things to keep in mind:

1. Success really can happen to anyone

It is easy to fall into the trap of thinking that successful people are somehow special, that they are a more extra-ordinary type of person, and that the world is divided into the kinds of people who are destined to be successful, and the rest.

But this is just not true. Successful people are just like

anyone else, except that they happen to have become successful. Success and achievement are doors that are open to anyone.

Sir Tom Stoppard did not have an easy start in life. He was born in Czechoslovakia and had to move countries several times with his family to escape German and Japanese invasions during the Second World War, during which time his father was killed. He moved to England at the age of nine. But when he wrote his play *Rosencrantz and Guildenstern Are Dead* at 29, he became the youngest ever playwright to have a play performed at the National Theatre in London. Both audiences and critics highly praised the play and Sir Tom has gone on to become one the UK's most acclaimed playwrights, with a fiftieth-anniversary production of *Rosencrantz and Guildenstern* performed at the Old Vic theatre, also in London.

Key to his success, he says, was his realisation that there was no reason why someone like him couldn't be successful.

He told the *Sunday Telegraph*, 'When I was starting off, the idea of having a play performed at the Old Vic was simply beyond one's dreams. And then when I found myself a few years later at the back of a theatre watching my play, looking around, it came to me as some form of revelation that the thing which I thought could only happen to truly extraordinary people – extraordinary writers and so on – actually happens to people like me. And it completely altered some perspective I had on who I was, in a rather healthy way. It was to do with understanding that I didn't actually need to be some sort of freak to be good enough for this to happen to me; I could just be what I was.'

2. A spirit of adventure will go a very long way

The single most useful thing to keep with you as you start playing to your strengths is a sense of adventure. This means being willing to try new things and seeing where they might lead, and being able to treat any setback as feedback rather than failure. Keep exploring and trying things out until you find something that fits you. And the good news is, you don't have to get it right first go. You've got time to experiment and try out different things.

It may be that having a single career isn't right for you, for example, and that you prefer to spend your life having a portfolio career made up of lots of different professions. Or it may be that you prefer to live in lots of different places rather than choosing just one. Or it could be that you spend different phases of your life pursuing very different goals – a few years spent working every hour and earning lots of money followed by time spent volunteering and pursuing the interests you love that don't make any money, perhaps. That's fine too. Life is not a single chapter, it is a book with lots of chapters, and you can make them as varied and exciting as you like.

Back in the 1970s there was a children's television show about a cartoon character called Mr Benn. At the start of every episode Mr Benn would set off from his house in a suit and bowler hat and visit a fancy dress shop. After exchanging a few words with the shopkeeper, he would step into a changing room and emerge with a different outfit on. Then he would go off and have an adventure, happy in the knowledge that however it turned out he could have a completely different outfit and a completely different adventure tomorrow.

That's the kind of approach that can take you a very long way.

3. Accept that you don't know everything right now

Just as you don't know everything in advance about a trip you are going to take, neither can you know everything about how your new life or career might unfold. But that's fine. You just have to treat it like doing a jigsaw: accept that the full picture is going to emerge gradually rather than instantly. While sometimes it will be straightforward to fit pieces together, at other times it will take more effort and patience. Sometimes you will find interesting pieces that open up a whole new section, and at other times you may find pieces that don't seem to belong anywhere right now. You just need to keep at it until the picture emerges and you can see clearly what you have achieved.

4. Realise that change doesn't have to be complicated

When you are contemplating making big changes in your life, it can be easy to imagine that the process of change is going to be incredibly complex. But it doesn't have to be. Sometimes it can be surprisingly simple.

When my friend Kate gave birth to a lovely baby boy she called him Liam and put his name on the birth certificate. But after a few weeks she realised she didn't like the name Liam after all, and decided that her baby didn't look like a Liam anyway. She began to wish she had called him Jack. In fact she wished it so much she started thinking that maybe she should have another baby boy and call that one Jack instead.

But fortunately Kate discovered you are allowed to add another first name to your baby's birth certificate, provided you do it within 12 months. So Liam became Jack and all was well.

Sometimes the idea of trying to change something can feel completely overwhelming, but when you take the time to look at it more closely, the steps to make that change happen and reach the solution are in fact very simple. The secret is to stay calm and find out as much information as you can about the change you want to make, before you begin. The more research you can do, the more likely you are to find a clear way out on the other side. You could ask a wise friend for advice, or you could ask Google. We are incredibly lucky to have the world's resources at our fingertips. Half an hour of typing questions into a search engine and following where the results lead can reveal all kinds of answers. At the very least, your search results will reveal websites, advice lines and organisations that could guide you.

5. Don't just follow the crowd

The world is full of people telling us what we should be thinking and wearing and saying and doing. We are constantly bombarded with advice from friends, newspapers, adverts and television programmes. And social media has made it worse, with everyone constantly sharing and blogging and opining and commenting. Indeed an entire section of the public relations industry is now devoted to the idea of 'thought leadership', in which business leaders and others write opinion pieces and blogs specifically designed to direct and guide your thoughts.

But just because everyone is shouting loudly doesn't make them right, and it doesn't mean you have to agree with them. Indeed, even if everyone else thinks one thing and you are the only one seeing it in a different way, you could still be right.

I have interviewed hundreds of successful entrepreneurs over the years and pretty much all of them have at some point had someone tell them that their business idea was crazy and would never work.

Have confidence in your own thoughts and ideas. Listen to other people's views, but then very consciously and deliberately set them to one side and make up your own mind.

6. Take up more room

Don't be meek. Meek is rubbish. You have just as much right to try to achieve great things as anyone else. Regular readers of my books will know I love swimming. I swim in my local pool every day if I can – I find it relaxing, calming and inspiring. Anyway, I arrived one morning to find two lanes set up as usual for lap swimmers; one for slow swimmers and one for fast. They were both empty – joy. I began swimming in the slow lane, then a man arrived and started swimming in the slow lane too. He was much faster than me. Meanwhile the fast lane was still completely empty. After a while the fast lane continued to be empty, and the fast-swimming man was still in my lane, so when he overtook me for the sixth time, I suggested that it would make more sense if he moved into the fast lane instead, then we could have a lane each to ourselves.

But instead he just smiled meekly and said, 'Oh no, I don't want to be greedy.' And continued swimming in the slow lane with me. But that's not being greedy, that's just being silly. It's not like he was eating someone else's bit of cake. The other lane was completely empty. No one else was using it, and he would have had a much nicer swim if he hadn't had to keep overtaking me every five minutes. In the end I moved into the fast lane myself.

Spread out and allow yourself some space. You have every right to be here. Get your own lane.

7. Understand that talent may not come fully formed

There is a pernicious idea that if you have to work hard at something, then you can't be any good at it; that your talent has to somehow appear fully formed and completely brilliant, without any effort on your part; that only natural talent counts. But this is nonsense. Talent very rarely exists purely in isolation; you need to craft it and shape it and polish it and work at it in order to make it shine. You need to put the effort in.

Perhaps the most revealing account of this process was given by comedian Frank Skinner in his book *On the Road*, in which he explained how he created a successful stand-up routine to take to the Edinburgh Fringe Festival. Before arriving in Edinburgh, he spent the previous eight months testing out his jokes in 34 new-material slots in small comedy clubs around London, and then in 12 full-length solo shows.

After each show Frank would rate every joke and decide whether it was funny enough to stay in his routine. He had calculated that for a one-hour show he needed 144 jokes. He writes: 'After each gig I went through the night's set ticking the jokes that worked, crossing the jokes that failed and question-marking the ones that did neither. Sometimes a bit of rejigging promotes these latter gags into the ticks column, but they don't get many chances. They are on a yellow card. I would say that 80 per cent of question marks end up taking an early bath.'

It sounds utterly exhausting, but his efforts have paid off. Frank Skinner has had an extremely successful career as a comedian, packing out large venues and winning many awards, as well as being a chat-show host and a presenter for many radio and television shows.

8. Learn how to pivot

The concept of pivoting is very big among technology start-up businesses right now. It's the understanding that you might not get your business idea completely right first time and so may need to change it or rework it a bit as you go along to get to where you want to be. But that's okay. In fact, it's more than okay, because the reworked idea can often turn out to be even stronger than the original one.

Kevin Systrom and Mike Kreiger, the entrepreneurs who created Instagram, actually started out with an idea for creating an online check-in app called Burbn. But despite attracting some funding and a lot of publicity, their Burbn app did not gain many users. Kevin and Mike began analysing the user data and they realised that people were mainly using Burbn to take photos rather than to check into places. So they pivoted their original idea to create a photo-sharing app and called it Instagram.

As Kevin told a conference, 'I remember what I'll call "pivot day". We sat down and said "What are we going to work on next? How are we going to evolve this product into something millions of people will want to use? What is the one thing that makes this product unique and interesting?" '

Instagram was an instant success, attracting 25,000 users on its first day, and just two years later the two founders sold it to Facebook for US $1 billion.

The idea of pivoting is a useful one outside the world of technology start-ups too. Pivoting is about being flexible, open-minded and creative, and about being able to adapt to changing situations around you. While it is useful to have an idea of where you want to end up, it is also important to understand that there is more than one way to get there.

9. Remember that you always have choices

It is surprisingly easy to forget this. You can get so used to doing the same thing, day in day out, that it becomes hard to remember there are other options. Back in the 1970s an airline called British Caledonian ran a long-running advertising campaign on television with the tagline, 'We never forget you have a choice.' Many of the adverts are extremely dated now, and the airline itself is long gone, but the tagline is still an immensely powerful one.

You too must never forget that you have choices, in every area of your life. You don't have to keep going along a path that isn't taking you where you want to be, you don't have to keep plugging away at a job or career you hate. There are always other options, lots of them, even if it might require a bit of effort to see what they are.

10. Go for it

Now that you know you can achieve more than you thought, you can let your ideas and imagination float free. Try whatever you want. Your dreams can be anything you want them to be. Not long ago there was a series on BBC Television called *The Life Swap Adventure*, in which people from the UK swapped lives with someone elsewhere in the world for a week to see what they could both learn from each other. An IT consultant from Essex swapped lives with a subsistence farmer from Malawi, for example, and a fisherwoman from a tiny village in Lancashire swapped lives with a successful businesswoman from Taiwan. But the real revelation of the series was not just that these people were all living such different lives; it was the realisation that there are so many different lives to choose from. You could live a completely different kind of life every week for a year and still hardly scratch the surface. The only tragedy is that we don't have enough time to live that many lives.

Chapter 14

What now?

'Give me a place to stand and I will move the world'

Archimedes, inventor and mathematician

For many years there was a widespread belief that humans use only 10 per cent of their brains. It is thought to have started with the US psychologist and philosopher William James, who in 1908 wrote that we 'are making use of only a small part of our possible mental and physical resources'. The notion was reinforced in 1936 when journalist Lowell Thomas wrote in the preface to Dale Carnegie's book *How to Win Friends and Influence People* that 'the average person develops only 10 per cent of his latent mental ability'.

It was an immensely appealing thought; the idea that if people wanted to achieve more in life, all they needed to do was switch on their 90 per cent of unused brain power and off they'd go. Sadly, however, it turns out not to be true after all. It's nothing more than an urban myth. Scientists have scanned the brain using magnetic resonance imaging and found that in reality there are no unused parts. You already use all 100 per cent of it.

But that's fine, because that's actually all you need.

Hopefully, this book has helped you see that you don't need any more brain power, or indeed any more anything, because you already have everything you need to be brilliant in work and life. All you need to do is to start playing to your strengths, and to get excited about what lies ahead.

Many years ago when I was about to leave university, I was feeling a bit anxious about what the future might hold. A good friend leant over to me and said simply: 'See how far you can go.' So now I pass on the same advice to you. See how far you can go. Because it's all out there waiting for you.

Good luck and please do stay in touch. Whatever stage you are at in getting to where you want to be, I would be delighted to hear from you. You can contact me via Twitter on @rachelbridge100, by email on rachel@rachelbridge.com, or via my website www.rachelbridge.com.

Acknowledgements

I would like to thank all the people I interviewed for this book for generously sharing their thoughts and stories. I would also like to thank Robert Dudley, Zoe Bohm and the fantastic team at Little, Brown for giving me the opportunity to write this book. Finally, once again a big thank you to my family for their support, and a massive hug to Harry and Jack for making every day brilliant.

Index

A

Access to Medicine 165
Acton, Brian 120
adventure holidays 48
Afghanistan 20
Al Fresco 141
Ali, Muhammad 101
Alive, Alive Oh! (Athill) 74
Alliance Manchester Business
    School 105
Amazon 114
André Deutsch 74
Apple 23
    and Blue Sky 91
Archer, Jeffrey 52
Archimedes 179
areas of life, questioning 9–10
Aristotle 39
assets, effective use of 80–1
Athill, Diana 74
Atkinson, Rowan 20

B

Backpacker Granny 11–12
backpacking 11–12
BAFTAs 47
Barnes, Natasha 107

Bartlett, Steve 89, 90
Battersea Dogs & Cats 83
BBC Monitoring Unit 12
beermaking 17
Bloom & Wild 126–7
Boaty McBoatface 119–20
Bock, Laszlo 91
Bonnes Vacances (Millard) 155
brain, use of 179
Branson, Richard 84
Braund, Lisa 46–7
Brighton Medical School 165
Brin, Sergey 90–1
British Caledonian 177
British Council:
        programmes in several
            countries run by 14
        scholarships 12
British Dyslexia Association 85
Bunton, Emma 93
Burbn 176

C

Canvas Holidays 141
career goals 8
Carnegie, Dale 57, 179
Cats Protection 83

Cavendish, Dominic 107
Central European University 74
changing direction 19–22
    from comedy to serious plays 20–1
Channel 4 46, 48, 128
Channel 5 81
character strengths 41 (*see also* strengths)
Cher 93
choosing your own timing 29–31
Church, Charlotte 93
Citizens Advice 50
Clarkson, Jeremy 150
Clos Lucé 137
Clothier, Pip 154–5
Cocorose London 65–6
The Collector (Naylor) 21
comedy writing 20
communication strengths 40 (*see also* strengths)
Companies House 149
Confucius 7
Connolly, Cyril 75
Coomber, Elaine 164–5
creative goals 9
creative play 90–2
creative strengths 40 (*see also* strengths)
crowdfunding 82–3 (*see also* money)
Cumming, Laura 106

D

da Vinci, Leonardo 137–8
Daily Mail 32, 73
Daily Telegraph 32, 107
D'Aloisio, Nick 73
DDI 1

Deci, Edward 18
Desert Island Discs 128
Desperate Housewives 137
different thinking 101–9
    and bigger picture 102–3
    and distractions 104
    and getting organised 105
    and looking outwards 105
    and making every day count 108–9
    and negativity, stamping on 104
    and priorities 106
    and seizing the moment 107
    taking action 109
direction:
    and assessing your reactions 10–12
    changing without fear 19–21
    and current surroundings, looking beyond 15–17
    and exploring your interests 12–14
    facing in right one 7–22
        taking action 22
    and goal, underpinning 17–18 (*see also* goals)
    and goals 8–9 (*see also* goals)
    and going back to basics 8
    and job shadowing 14–15
    owing 19
    and questioning things 9–10
Disability Rights UK 85
DisabilityJobSite 85

Discovery 119
Doherty, Fraser 69–70
Domaine du Merchien
    vineyard 17
Dragon's Den 166
Dropbox 100
Dude Perfect 27–8
Dunlop, Fuchsia 12–14
    books by 13
Dyer, Geoff 153
dyslexia 84
Dyson, James 131–2

E

e-books 113–14
East London Late Starters
    Orchestra 161
Eat Pray Love (Gilbert) 55
Edinburgh Fringe 21, 139–40,
    175
education, and wearing
    slippers, not shoes 33
Einstein, Albert 121, 140
EmployAbility 85
Endemol 47
enjoying what you do 27–9
Ephron, Nora 95
ER 137
Ernest Shackleton 119
E6PR 144
The Estate Series (Sherratt) 113
E.T. the Extra-Terrestrial 121
Eurocamp 141
Eurostar 140–1
Evans, Andy 89–90
Eventbrite 80
Everest Base Camp 48
excitement, *see* getting excited
Exodus 48
exploring interests 12–14

F

Facebook 36, 120, 140, 149, 176
Family Matters 137
Financial Times 163
Findern Primary School 33
first step, taking 135–45
    and identifying audience
        139–40
    and keeping flame
        burning 142
    and setting something
        different in motion
        140–1
    and signposts 142–3
    and starting ball rolling
        136–7
    taking action 145
    without limits 143–4
Floodlight 54, 92
Floyd, Keith 124–5
Forbes 152
Forster, Geraldine 11–12
free technology 80
Fringe First award 21
Funny Girl 107

G

Gallagher, Tony 32
gap year 29–30
Gap Years for Grown Ups 31
Gap360 31
Gardetta, Jo 30
Gelbard, Aron 125–7
Gervaise, Ricky 73
Get Into Teaching 164
getting excited 159–67
    and adventure 159–60
    and leadership skills 162
    (*see also* leadership and
        management)

getting excited – *continued*
   and making a difference
      163
   and new skills 161–2
   and pioneering 160–1
   and something
      completely different
      163–4
   and standing out 166
   taking action 167
   and things that matter to
      you 164–5
Gilbert, Elizabeth 55
Girl Guides and Scouts 162
Glasgow Rangers 152
goals:
   and basics, asking
      yourself about 8
   career 8
   creative 9
   lifestyle 9
   personal 9
   purpose-driven and
      profit-led 18
   setting route for, *see* map:
      drawing your own
   underpinning 17–18
   university research into
      18
   work 9
GoDaddy 149
good habits 87–100
   and allowing magic to
      happen 99–100
   and being less predictable
      95–6
   and change as new
      routine 88–9
   and channelling Ephron
      95
   and creative play 90–2
   and extra effort 89–90

   and gathering allies
      92–4
   and quiet times 96–7
   and stuff you hate,
      ditching 98–9
   taking action 100
   and upside 97–8
Goodwin, Phil 20
Google, and employees'
   creative projects 90–1
Guardian 32, 130
gut instinct 118–19

H

habits, good, *see* good habits
Hall, Michelle 33
Halloween 98–9
Hastings, Scott 111–12
Havas Worldwide 96–7
Haworth, Ian 143
Hiscox 154
Holly and Co 118
Home Exchange 80
Housesitters 80–1
*How to Win Friends and
   Influence People*
   (Carnegie) 179
Hubud 44
human brain, use of 179
Huxley, Aldous 148
Hynes, Jayne 75–6

I

I to I 81
ICL 116
imaginative strengths 40
   (*see also* strengths)
Indeed 83
Indiegogo 82
Instagram 149, 176

Intellectual Property Office 149

interests, exploring 12–14

Iraq 21

The Island with Bear Grylls 48

ITV 48

J

James Clark Ross 119

James Cook 119

James, William 179

Jane (author's friend) 26

Jaws 121

Jenkins, Katherine 93

job shadowing 14–15

    Viewvo service for 15

Jobs, Steve 23–4, 123

Jobs for the Girls 161

Joe and Caspar's Road Trip USA 19

John, Elton 93

Joosten, Kathryn 136–7

Jordan, Michael 67, 159

Julie (author's friend) 142

Jurassic Park 121

K

Kabul 20

Kane and Abel (Archer) 52, 53

Kate (author's friend) 172–3

KDP 114

Kellaway, Lucy 163

Kellogg, John 98

Kempson, Dick 159–60

Kentucky Fried Chicken 73

Kickstarter 82

Kiddyum 76

Kidzania 7

Kierkegaard, Søren 135

Kindle 113

Kreiger, Mike 176

L

La Tante Claire 152

Lady Gaga 121

Lawrence, D.H. 153

LCN 149

leadership and management 49, 50, 59, 162

Lee, Aileen 100

Lee, Caspar 19

Leo, Janan 64–6

Lewis, Michael 97

Liar's Poker (Lewis) 97

The Life Swap Adventure 177–8

lifestyle goals 9

Lings Cars 166

M

McCall, Davina 101–2

McKinsey 162

magazines, ideas from 34

magic ingredients 123–33

    ambition 129–31

        synonyms for 129

    determination 131–3

        synonyms for 131

    enthusiasm 124–5

        synonyms for 124

    imagination 125–7

        synonyms for 125

    optimism 127–9

        synonyms for 127

    taking action 133

magistrates 141

MailChimp 80

Manchester Business Centre 105

Manchester University 105

map:
  drawing your own 23–37
    and choosing your
      timing 29–31
    and enjoying 27–9
    and mission statement
      34–5, 36
    and others' ideas 33–4
    and prize, keeping eye
      on 35–6
    and reading your
      actions 26–7
    starting with blank
      sheet 24–6
    taking action 36–7
    and what others
      think 31–2
Mark (author's friend) 43
Maxus 130
Meakin, David 15–17
  first wine vintage of 17
Meakin, Sarah 16–17
  first wine vintage of 17
Medical Schools Council
  165
Medicine Foundation 165
Melody Maker 128
Messi, Lionel 156
Michael Page 83
Microsoft, and Garage 91
Millard, Rosie 154–5
Milne, A.A. 1
mission statement, writing
  34–5, 36 (*see also* map:
  drawing your own)
Mr Benn 171
momentum 135
  and starting ball rolling
    136–7
Mona Lisa (da Vinci) 138
money:
  and creative thinking 79

and crowdfunding 82–3
and earning while
  learning 81–2
and effective use of assets
  80–1
and free technology 80
getting to grips with
  78–9
tempting to blame lack
  of 78
Moneyball (Lewis) 97
MoneySavingExpert 78
Monroe, Marilyn 121
Moran, Caitlin 128
Moro 32
Mycoskie, Blake 163

N

National Bureau of Economic
  Research 128
National Council for
  Voluntary Organisations
  50
National Environment
  Research Council 119
National Museum of Science
  and Media 138–9
National Theatre 170
Naylor, Henry 20–1
  more plays from 21
negativity, stamping on 104
Nerf 28
New Covent Garden 125–6
New Lives in the Wild 81
NICEIC 161
Nobel Prize for Physics 121
*Not a Penny More, Not a Penny
  Less* (Archer) 52
NotontheHighStreet.com
  118
NowTeach 163–4

O

obstacles 2–3, 67–86
   and age 73–4
   creating advantages from
     3, 68–9
   and knowing right people
     71–2
   and lack of knowledge or
     experience 69–70
   and money 78–83
     creative thinking 79
     crowdfunding 82–3
     earning while learning
      81–2
     effective use of assets
      80–1
     free technology 80
     getting to grips with
      78–9
   and personal
     circumstances 83–5
   taking action 85–6
   and young family 75–7
Ocado 76
The Office 73
Old Vic 170
Olympic Games 130
Open University 54
organisational strengths 40
   (*see also* strengths)
Otago, University of 92
others' ideas, adapting 33–4
others' stories, your reactions
   to 10–12
Out of Sheer Rage (Dyer) 153

P

Page, Larry 90–1
Page, Michael 83
Parsons, Andy 20

*Parsons and Naylor's Pull-Out
   Sections* 20
Pattison, Lindsay 130
Pennsylvania, University of
   129
people strengths 40 (*see also*
   strengths)
personal goals 9

Philip, King 106
Pinterest 149
pioneering 160–1
powerful ideas 169–78
   acceptance, that you
     don't know everything
     172
   change doesn't have to be
     complicated 172–3
   choices 177
   going for it 177–8
   not just following the
     crowd 173–4
   pivoting 176–7
   spirit of adventure 170–1
   success is for anyone
     169–70
   taking up more room
     174–5
   talent may not come fully
     formed 175–6
practical strengths 40
   (*see also* strengths)
Pressat 73
Prince's Trust 85
Pringles 28
problem-solving strengths 40
   (*see also* strengths)
Pyke, Julia 81

Q

questioning 9–10

R

Raised by Wolves 128
Ramsay, Gordon 152
reality, maintaining 147–57
    and contingency plans
      152
    and embracing your
      restrictions 153
    and flexibility 149–50
    and getting basic in place
      148–9
    and starting at bottom
      151
    and staying clear-eyed
      154
    and success on its own
      terms 155–6
    taking action 157
    and what you've got,
      working with 154–5
redundancy 154
Reed 49
Regency House Party 46–7
Rhys Jones, Griff 20
Rightmove 81
On the Road (Skinner) 175
Roadnight, Graham 88–9
ROAR 93
Rochester, University of 18
Roosevelt, Theodore 147
Roseanne 137
*Rosencrantz and Guildenstern
    are Dead* (Stoppard) 170
Royal Caribbean 25
Royal Research vessels 119

S

Sainsbury's 76
Salcedo, Mario 25–6
Salt Water Brewery, Florida 144
Samaritans 50

Sanders, Colonel 73
School of Life 54
Scotsman 21
Scouts and Girl Guides 162
Season Workers 141
Seligman, Martin 129
Shalit, Jonathan 93–4
Shall We Tell the President?
    (Archer) 52
Shand, Wendy 71–2
*Shark's Fin and Sichuan
    Pepper* (Dunlop) 13
Shaw, George Bernard 23
Sherratt, Mel 112–13
shoes, not wearing in school
    33
Shone, Gareth 81
Sichuan Cookery (Dunlop)
    13
Sichuan University,
    Chengdu 12
Sichuanese cuisine 13
Silkwood 95
Sinatra, Dr Roberta 73–4
Sir David Attenborough 120
Skinner, Frank 175–6
Skyscanner 100
Sleepless in Seattle 95
Smith, Mel 20
Smith, Sheridan 107
Snapchat 100
Social Chain 89–90
Sony 34
Southern California,
    University of 121
Spielberg, Steven 121
Spitting Image 20
Stanway, Ben 125–7
Starbucks 34
The Steps to Work 49
Stevenson, Robert Louis 87
Stoppard, Tom 170

strengths:
  in both work and life 4
  identifying 39–56
    and applying effort
      51–3
    asking others 41–2
    boosting best bits 51
    by challenging yourself
      46–7
    and continued learning
      53–4
    and knowing what you
      seek 40–1
    and old school reports
      42–3
    and persisting 55
    reconfiguring negative
      traits 45–6
    and space to think
      43–4
    taking action 56
    and transferable skills
      48–9
    and volunteering 49–50
  and improving how you
    feel 3
  playing to 3
  types of 40–1
Strictly Ballroom 111–12
Suggs, Joe 19
Summly 73
Sunday Telegraph 170
Sunday Times 72, 84
SuperJam 70
Systrom, Kevin 176

T

taking action:
  different thinking 109
    (*see also* different
      thinking)

direction 22
  (*see also* direction)
first step, taking 145
  (*see also* first step,
    taking)
getting excited 167 (*see*
  also getting excited)
good habits 100 (*see also*
  good habits)
magic ingredients 133 (*see*
  also magic ingredients)
map 36–7 (*see also* map)
obstacles 85–6 (*see also*
  obstacles)
reality, maintaining
  157 (*see also* reality,
    maintaining)
strengths 56
work 66 (*see also* work)
taking control 111–21
  and doing it yourself
    112–24
  and going direct 114–16
  and gut instinct 118–19
  and living your life for
    you 116–18
  and own decisions
    119–20
  and rejection seen as
    motivation 120–1
  taking action 121
Taliban 20
Taunting the Dead (Sherratt)
  113, 114
technical or technological
  strengths 40 (*see also*
  strengths)
TED talks 54, 55
TEFL 81
Texas A&M University 27
This Time Next Year 101–2
Thomas, Lowell 179

Thompson, Chris 44
Time Out 13
Times 21, 72, 128, 151
timing, your own 29–31
TOMS 163
Toney, Tyler 28
Total Jobs 105
Tots to Travel 72
traits, negative, reconfiguring
    45–6
transferable skills 48–9
Travellers Worldwide 31
Trusted House Sitters 80–1
Tucker, Holly 118–19
Turner, James 83

U

UCAS 74

V

Valentine, Ling 166
The Vanishing Man (Cumming)
    106
Vaughan, Andy 116–18
Velázquez, Diego 106
Viewvo 15
Virgin group 84
Virgin Media 115
Virgin Trains 65, 66
Vitruvian Man (da Vinci) 138
Vogue 121
The Voice 48
volunteering 49–50
Volunteers Week 50
VSO 81

W

Waitrose 70
war correspondents 20

We Believers 144
Wesley, Mary 73
West, Mae 169
The West Wing 137
WhatsApp 120
When Harry Met Sally 95
WHSmith 34
wikiHow 71
winemaking 16–17
Winnie the Pooh (Milne) 1
Wintour, Anna 121
Women on the Tools 161
work:
        from aboard cruise liner,
            see Salcedo, Mario
        and basics, asking
            yourself about 8
        best achievement of,
            deciding 57–66
        boredom with 1
        and changing direction
            19–22
        and digital nomads 58
        as employee 58, 59–61
            and adaptability 60
            and communication
                skills 60
            key strengths for 59–61
            and leadership and
                management skills
                59
            and reliability 59
            and staying calm 60–1
            and team work 60
        flexible arrangements for
            57
        hybrid option – for both
            self and employer 58–9,
            63–6
            and discipline 64
            and focus 63–4
            key strengths for 63–6

and realistic
expectations 64
and time-management
64–6
and job shadowing 14–15
Viewvo service for 15
and looking beyond
current surroundings
15–17
and redundancy 154
for self 58, 61–3
key strengths for 61–3
and knowledge 62
and organisational
skills 62
and resilience 63
and self-determination
62–3
and self-discipline 61
and self-motivation 61
and setting your route,

see map: drawing your
own
taking action 66
technology brings
flexibility to 4, 57
and trying out
alternatives 8
work goals 9
'The World's Longest
Basketball Shot' 28
WPP 143
Wunderman 143

Y

Youth Hostel Association 48
YouTube 90, 149
Creator Academy set up
by 29
Dude Perfect 27–8
Suggs and Lee 19